# A COMPARATIVE VIEW

OF THE

# CONSTITUTIONS OF GREAT BRITAIN

AND THE

# UNITED STATES OF AMERICA,

IN SIX LECTURES.

By P. F. AIKEN, Advocate.

"If circumspection and caution are a part of wisdom, when we work only upon inanimate matter, surely they become a part of duty too, when the subject of our demolition and construction is not brick and timber, but sentient beings, by the sudden alteration of whose state, condition, and habits, multitudes may be rendered miserable."

BURKE.

THE LAWBOOK EXCHANGE, LTD.
Clark, New Jersey

ISBN 9781584779476 (hardcover)
ISBN 9781616191733 (paperback)

Lawbook Exchange edition 2011

*The quality of this reprint is equivalent to the quality of the original work.*

## THE LAWBOOK EXCHANGE, LTD.

33 Terminal Avenue
Clark, New Jersey 07066-1321

*Please see our website for a selection of our other publications
and fine facsimile reprints of classic works of legal history:*
www.lawbookexchange.com

### Library of Congress Cataloging-in-Publication Data

Aiken, P. F. (Peter Freeland)
  A comparative view of the constitutions of Great Britain and the
United States of America, in six lectures / by P.F. Aiken.
    p. cm.
  Originally published: London : Longman and Co., 1842.
  Includes bibliographical references.
  ISBN-13: 978-1-58477-947-6 (cloth : alk. paper)
  ISBN-10: 1-58477-947-0 (cloth : alk. paper)
  1. Constitutional law--United States. 2. Constitutional law--
Great Britain. 3. United States--Politics and government. 4.
Great Britain--Politics and government. I. Title.
  KF4554.A35 2009
  342.41--dc22                          2008047179

*Printed in the United States of America on acid-free paper*

# A COMPARATIVE VIEW

OF THE

## CONSTITUTIONS OF GREAT BRITAIN

AND THE

## UNITED STATES OF AMERICA,

IN SIX LECTURES.

By P. F. AIKEN, ADVOCATE.

"If circumspection and caution are a part of wisdom, when we work only upon inanimate matter, surely they become a part of duty too, when the subject of our demolition and construction is not brick and timber, but sentient beings, by the sudden alteration of whose state, condition, and habits, multitudes may be rendered miserable."

BURKE.

LONDON:

LONGMAN AND CO.; HAMILTON, ADAMS, AND CO.

BRISTOL: STRONG. — EDINBURGH: BLACKWOOD AND SON. —

DUBLIN: MILLIKEN AND CO.

1842.

# CONTENTS.

___

## LECTURE I.

### INTRODUCTORY.

## LECTURE II.

### PROVINCIAL INSTITUTIONS—OUTLINE OF AMERICAN CONSTITUTION.

## CONTENTS.

### LECTURE III.

ELECTIVE FRANCHISE—LEGISLATIVE ASSEMBLIES.

### LECTURE IV.

THE EXECUTIVE POWER.

### LECTURE V.

LAW—RELIGION.

### LECTURE VI.

SOCIAL INFLUENCE OF POLITICAL INSTITUTIONS.

# PREFACE.

———

THESE discourses were originally prepared for a literary association at Bristol, designed chiefly for the improvement of young men, by means of a select library, and lectures given by clergymen and gentlemen who take an interest in the institution. The author was afterwards invited to deliver them elsewhere; and to the numerous and most respectable audience, at whose request they are published, he has to apologize for the delay caused by his acceptance of an invitation from the principal inhabitants of Newport, in Monmouthshire, to repeat the course there, at the close of autumn. But he has thus been enabled to extend and illustrate it, by a reference to recent documents and very important events.

Great Britain and America having been reunited in amicable bonds, every sincere patriot and philanthropist will desire that their concord may be perpetual, and will mingle his aspirations for the welfare of both countries.

An Englishman, how careful soever, to derive his knowledge of the institutions of the United States, from the best sources, should be apprehensive of error. But having thus endeavoured to guard against fallacy, it is his privilege to state unreservedly his honest convictions.

The author's design was, to compare our limited monarchy with the greatest modern republic, not in order to disparage either, but to elucidate both to a popular audience of his own countrymen. That plan would have circumscribed the limits of this work, even had he possessed the leisure and the ability to execute it in a manner more worthy of the theme. But in its present form, it may perhaps be read by those to whom a more costly and elaborate treatise would not be accessible.

The subject has an intrinsic claim to attention. It embraces a variety of topics, both entertaining and important, and historical truths of immense practical value, concerning which the people are deeply interested and too often misled.

These pages are especially dedicated to the youth and to the working classes of this kingdom. May they be happy in justly appreciating our national institutions, in cherishing true liberty and rejecting its counterfeits.

CLIFTON, 13th December, 1842.

# INTRODUCTORY.

## LECTURE I.

Discovery of America and contemporaneous events—Common origin of the British and American people and their institutions—Primitive character of the colonists and their final separation from the mother country—important *differences* in the condition of the two nations—The American constitution was planned by Congress, is a legislative experiment, and is not a precedent to be followed by this country.

THE invention of printing, the Reformation, and the discovery of America, occurring in the order of Divine Providence very near the same period, combined to produce the most important and beneficial results to mankind. The art of printing, by which thought is transmitted rapidly and extensively from mind to mind and from age to age, performed its noblest office as an auxiliary to the Reformation. And after the Reformation had made considerable progress, the religious differences which arose in England, led many of our ancestors to seek an asylum in the recently-discovered continent of North America. Thither they carried the reformed doctrines, which are now professed by millions of their descendants in the new world, and are propagated by their missionaries in various parts of the globe.

B

The discovery of America tended, in connection with other causes, to render the moderns more original and more independent of antiquity. It opened a wide field for geographical and scientific discovery, for mercantile adventure, and daring enterprise. To the young, the hopeful, the disappointed, the ambitious, America was a land of promise, and for many generations innumerable emigrants from the civilized societies of the old world, have started forward in that ample region, in a new and more prosperous course. The Anglo-American colonies especially, have immensely extended commerce and manufactures, have changed the distribution of wealth, and modified the influence of hereditary rank and fortune in the parent state. Their successful struggle for independence had an important bearing on the political condition of European kingdoms; and to Englishmen especially, the study of their history and institutions is essential, and full of the most interesting and valuable instruction.

The American continent extends almost from pole to pole; its loftiest mountains surpass the highest Alps; its lakes, resembling inland seas, supply the mightiest rivers of the earth; its immense plains of exhaustless fertility yield the various productions of tropical and temperate regions; and its climate is generally far more favourable to man than that of Asia or of Africa. Such is the magnificent abode prepared from the beginning by the all-bountiful Creator, but which was reserved till these latter days, to receive the overflowing population of the ancient kingdoms of the earth.

The first settlers on the shores of the Antilles and of South America, were gladdened by the discovery of islands of extraordinary beauty, in a sea calm, clear, and sparkling beneath the glowing sky of the tropics. The peaceful inhabitants of that paradise of the South were soon subdued and enslaved, and were forced by their avaricious conquerors to toil and perish in the mines. The colonists themselves soon became enervated and debased, and the treasures of gold and silver which they obtained by so many and so cruel wrongs, brought with them a curse. Impoverished Spain has lost her South American colonies by revolt; and those young republics, the æra of whose independence it was confidently foretold would be the commencement of a bright period of prosperity, of glory, and of happiness, have ever since their separation from the mother country been the theatre of revolutions, assassinations, and civil wars, which have disappointed the ardent hopes that were entertained of their rising greatness.

Between the Atlantic and the eastern base of the Alleghany mountains, whose mean distance from the sea is about one hundred miles, the bleak and barren shores of New England extend for nine hundred miles. On that inhospitable coast the first settlers from England landed. Rocks and gloomy forests seemed to bar their way. Farther inland lay a wilderness, inhabited by tribes of warlike savages, where alternate vegetation and decay had for ages been preparing a richly productive soil for the plough. The great valley which lies between the eastern and western range of the mountains of North America, comprehends a space of one million three hundred and forty-two thousand square miles, being twenty-six times larger than England and Wales. Through that valley the majestic Mississippi takes its course of two thousand five hundred miles, having a mean depth of fifteen feet, even at the distance of one thousand three hundred and sixty miles from its mouth. The Rhine and the Danube are streamlets in comparison with that mighty river, whose descriptive Indian name is the "Father of waters." Fifty-seven great navigable rivers pour their tributary waters into its tide, and of these, the Missouri flows about two thousand five hundred miles, the Arkansas one thousand three hundred miles, the Red River one thousand miles. To the west of the Mississippi the woods disappear, and there are plains of unknown extent.

If the first British settlers on the American continent had quitted their native country, either at an earlier and less enlightened period of our history, or in the present age, doubtless the character of the American people and of their institutions, would have been materially different from what they became. The colonies in New England were the *exemplar of all the rest,* and the *primitive character* of the colonists *was derived from that of the mother country at the time of their departure.* It is therefore important to advert briefly to the state of society in England at that period, and subsequent to the Reformation.

The great social changes of former times were generally produced by conquest, the arts of human policy, the struggles of men for power, wealth, glory, or freedom. The Reformation was a revolution caused by the powerful influence of *truth.* It gave an impulse to society which will be felt to the end of time. Several devout and humble men, in different parts of Europe, were almost simultaneously led to perceive scriptural truths, that had long been corrupted and concealed. The great theme of revelation filled their souls,—inspired them with fervent zeal and lofty courage. Their words, instinct with life and power, were eloquent to stir men's deepest and strongest feelings of attachment or of enmity. Their adversaries were confident in their numbers, in their secular and ecclesiastical power, in their scholastic theology, and controversial skill; but they could not resist nor gainsay the spirit and wisdom of the first Reformers, who believed and taught the pure gospel, who suffered, who died for it, and have

handed down to us that precious treasure and inheritance, with liberty of conscience and freedom of thought.

Many of the kings of Europe combined with the
Pope to arrest the progress of the Reformation
in their dominions, by force. In that design they
were permitted to succeed. But none may reject the
truth with impunity : and doubtless those kingdoms
would have made far higher attainments, and would
have enjoyed greater and more uninterrupted happiness,
if Christianity had shed its purest light over all Europe.
For it is to a Reformation confined to a *part* only of
Europe, that we owe our deliverance from the spiritual
and intellectual bondage of the dark ages. The Reformation, although it was partial and limited in its
operation, did bring glorious light and liberty. Touched
by its rays, genius and talents of the highest order
sprung up in exuberant fertility, and the long imprisoned currents of thought and of enterprise flowed
afresh. In England especially, the remarkable change
resembled the return of spring after a long polar winter,
when the renovated earth suddenly teems with luxuriant
vegetation, and the frozen streams gush out, and sparkle
in perpetual day.

It was not until Elizabeth ascended the throne, that
the Reformation was established, either in England or
in Scotland. Now, from the middle of her reign till
about a century afterwards, is an unrivalled historical
period, surpassing the best days of Greece, the Augus-
tan age of Rome, the times of the Medici in modern
Italy, the age of Louis the Fourteenth in France, and
that of Queen Anne in England. The illustrious men
of that time were of vast capacity and creative genius,
who made large additions to science, or produced literary works of high and enduring excellence. Bacon,
who prepared the way for all the great discoveries of modern times ; Spenser, Shakspere, and Milton ; Barrow

and Jeremy Taylor, Cudworth and Hobbes, Drake,
Raleigh, Sydney, Coke, and Selden, Harvey, Napier,
and Buchanan, — whose memorable names suggest
some of the highest attainments of the human mind,
in poetry, theology, philosophy, law, science, and literature.   Nor should we omit to mention the publication
of the first English newspaper, in Queen Elizabeth's
reign,—the origin of a power of immense efficacy, both
for good and for evil.

Whoever would desire to know some of the best and
brightest thoughts of English writers, expressed in the
full energy and beauty of our language, must study the
writings of the century succeeding the Reformation.
One noble and invaluable specimen of the pure racy
English style of the men of those days is in the hands
of all—the translation of the Bible.

From the bosom of a society so far advanced in
knowledge and civilization, so rich in genius, so characterised by masculine vigour and by the unmixed
peculiarities of our nation ; containing so much matured
excellence, and so many germs of future greatness, the
first British colonists of North America went forth.

Queen Elizabeth gave a name to Virginia, but no
permanent colony was established during her reign.
In the year 1607 a small band of emigrants landed
there.   They were of the higher order of society in
England, and members of the Established Church,
and were accompanied by an exemplary and esteemed
clergyman. Religious considerations had induced them
to quit their native country; and they described their
settlement on a continent, inhabited by wild Indians,
as a work " which by the providence of God might
tend to the glory of his Divine Majesty, and the propagating of the Christian religion."   They soon built
an episcopal church, on a peninsula which projects
from the northern shore of James' River.   Its ruins,

and the tombs around it, still remain,—the only memorial of Jamestown, the first English settlement in
the New World.

The first settlers in New England landed thirteen
years afterwards. The greater part of them were
neither of the aristocratic nor of the lower and poorer
class, but they were educated persons of the middle
ranks of English society, sober, industrious, devout,
and strictly moral. That system of local government in parishes and towns, which originated with our
Saxon ancestors, and lies at the foundation of British
liberty, then existed in considerable perfection in
England. During the long-continued political con-
tests of those times, the colonists had gained an expe-
rimental knowledge of the principles of civil liberty;
and the tendency of their political opinions was towards
republicanism. Religion was a subject of earnest consideration with them, and they had taken a deep interest
in the theological controversies of that period. The
settlers in New England were Puritans, a name given
to them on account of the severity of their manners,
and their claims to strict purity of worship and discipline. There was a stern sincerity in their attachment
to their opinions, which almost amounted to bigotry.
They were ready to suffer for conscience sake; and in the
school of adversity they had learned to value the rights
of conscience, and to know something of the principles
of toleration. They derived the elements of civil and
religious liberty from the institutions of their native
country. But having been oppressed and persecuted,
they forsook their homes, and with their families they
sought independence in the savage deserts of North
America.

> What sought they thus afar ?
> Bright jewels of the mine—

The wealth of seas—the spoils of war ?
They sought a faith's pure shrine.*

The Rev. Cotton Mather, an evangelical minister of
Boston, in his Ecclesiastical History of New England,

* "There was in the principles of the Puritans nothing of
philosophy, either in the good sense of the word or the bad.
And it is also most unjust to charge them with irreverence
or want of humility.  They received the scriptures as God's
word, and they followed them implicitly.  Neither do they
seem chargeable with establishing nice distinctions, in order
to evade their obvious meaning;  their fault seems rather to
have lain in the other extreme; they acquiesced in the obvious and literal meaning too unhesitatingly.  Nor yet were
they wanting in respect for all human authority, as trusting
in their own wisdom and piety only.  On the contrary, the
decisions of the earlier church with respect to the great
Christian doctrines, they received without questioning ; they
by no means took the scriptures into their hands, and sat
down to make a new creed of their own out of them.  They
disregarded the church only where the church departed from
the obvious sense of scripture ; I do not say the true sense,
but the obvious one.  The difference as to their moral character is considerable : because he who maintains another
than the obvious sense of scripture against other men, may
indeed be perfectly right, but he is liable to the charge,
whether grave or frivolous as it may be, of preferring his
own interpretation to that of the church.  But maintaining
the obvious sense, even if it be the wrong one, he can hardly
be charged himself with arrogance ; he may with greater
plausibility retort the charge on his opponents, that they
are substituting the devices of their own ingenuity for the
plain sense of the word of God. . . . . . . The Puritans wished
to alter the existing church system for one which they believed to be freer and better; and so far they resembled a
common popular party : but inasmuch as in this and all other
matters their great principle was conformity to scripture,
and they pushed this to an extravagant excess, because their
interpretation of scripture was continually faulty, there was,
together with their free political spirit, a narrow spirit in
things religious which shocked not only the popular party
of the succeeding age, but many even in their own day, who
politically entertained opinions far narrower than theirs."—
Dr. ARNOLD's *Introductory Lectures on Modern History*.

published in 1698, says:—"There were more than a few attempts of the English to people and improve the parts of New England which were to the northward of New Plymouth; but the designs of those attempts being aimed no higher than the advancement of some *worldly interests*, a constant series of disasters has confounded them, until thére was a plantation erected *upon the nobler designs of Christianity;* and that plantation, though it has had more adversaries than perhaps any upon earth, yet having obtained help from God, it continues to this day." The emigrants were about one hundred and fifty in number; and after an unfavourable and tempestuous voyage, they were compelled to land on that part of the New England coast, where the town of Plymouth is now built. The rock on which they landed is an object of great curiosity and veneration in the United States. As soon as they had landed they passed the following act:—" In the name of God, amen. We whose names are underwritten, the loyal subjects of our dread Sovereign Lord, King James, having undertaken, for the glory of God, and the advancement of the Christian faith, and the honour of our king and country, a voyage to plant the first colony in the northern parts of Virginia; do by these presents solemnly and mutually, in the presence of God and one another, covenant and combine ourselves together into a civil body politick, for our better ordering and preservation, and furtherance of the ends aforesaid," &c. This social contract was drawn up in 1620, and the emigrants who founded other settlements in New England, soon afterwards acted in a similar manner.

Never was a colony planted with less apparent prospect of success, but with higher and holier aims; and the result is a glorious and instructive lesson to nations: for may not the words of the inspired prophet be

applied historically to that people, " A little one shall
become a thousand, and a small one a strong nation.
I the Lord will hasten it in his time."

Let an American statesman, Mr. Everett, the present
ambassador to England from the United States, elo-
quently describe the humble origin and future greatness
of his country :—" Shut now the volume of history, and
tell me on any principle of *human* probability, what
shall be the fate of this handful of adventurers? Tell
me, man of military science, in how many months
were they all swept off by the thirty savage tribes enu-
merated within the early limits of New England? Tell
me, politician, how long did this shadow of a colony,
on which your conventions and treaties had not smiled,
languish on the distant coast? Student of history,
compare for me the baffled projects, the deserted settlements, the abandoned adventures of other times, and
find the parallel of this. Was it the winter's storm,
beating upon the houseless heads of women and children? was it hard labour and spare meals? was it disease? was it the tomahawk? was it the deep malady
of a blighted hope, a ruined enterprize, and a broken
heart, aching in its last moments at the recollection of
the loved and left beyond the sea? was it some, or all
of these united, that hurried this forsaken company to
their melancholy fate? And is it possible that neither
of these causes—that not all combined, were able to
blast this bud of hope? Is it possible that, from a beginning so feeble, so frail, so worthy not so much of
admiration as of pity, there has gone forth a progress
so steady, a growth so wonderful, a reality so important,
a promise yet to be fulfilled so glorious?"

The number of settlers increased by arrivals from
Europe almost every year. Rhode Island was purchased from the Indians about the year 1638. Connecticut, New Hampshire, and Maine were founded

soon afterwards. Hume the historian, in narrating the events of Charles the First's reign, in the year 1637, states that, " the Puritans, restrained in England, shipped themselves off for America, and laid there the foundations of a government, which possessed all the liberty, both civil and religious, of which they found themselves bereaved in their native country. But their enemies, unwilling that they should any where enjoy ease and contentment, and dreading perhaps the dangerous consequences of so disaffected a colony, prevailed on the king to issue a proclamation, debarring these devotees access even into those inhospitable deserts. Eight ships lying in the Thames, and ready to sail, were detained by order of council, and in these were: Sir Arthur Hazelrig, John Hambden, John Pym, and Oliver Cromwell, who had resolved for ever to abandon their native country." Hume quaintly observes, " The king had afterwards full leisure to repent this exercise of his authority." But the fact deserves more serious consideration, as one of those remarkable passages in history, which prove on what apparently trivial circumstances the most momentous results depend. The detention of those vessels by an arbitrary mandate, ultimately led to civil war and rebellion,—to the execution of the king himself,—to the overthrow of the monarchy,—to Cromwell's usurpation,—and to the manifold and important consequences which arose out of those memorable events.

The progress of emigration was not effectually checked by the order in council, for in the following year three thousand persons embarked for New England. The British government allowed the New England colonies to enjoy a large share of political independence, either under governors or chartered companies, or laws framed in general conformity with those of England, administered by themselves, under the protection of the mother

country.   The rights of personal liberty, trial by jury,
the voting of taxes by the people, and their intervention in public affairs, were recognized by the laws of
New England.   The great uniformity in opinions, and
the near approach to equality in condition, which
existed in those colonies, prepared them for democratic
institutions.   Their governors and other public functionaries were chosen by the people, and the elective
franchise was given in some of the states to the whole
of the citizens, and in all of them it was very extensively conferred.   Each town was a little republic,
although the supremacy of the mother country and the
authority of the British sovereign were acknowledged.
But the colonists were accustomed to believe that their
local assemblies stood in the same relation to them as
the British parliament did to the parent state.   In
several branches of useful legislation, those colonies
were in advance of all the states of Europe at that day.
Their regulations for the relief of the poor, for public
registers, for the maintenance of roads, and above all
for education, were excellent.   Schools were established
in every township, and in the more populous districts;
and the inhabitants were required, under a penalty, to
support them.   The language of their enactments de-
notes the serious and devout spirit in which they were
framed; with reference to which M. De Tocqueville
remarks: " In America *religion* was the road to knowledge, and the observance of the *divine laws* led man
to civil freedom."

New York, originally a Dutch settlement and founded
about the year 1614, was afterwards taken and established by the English.   New Jersey was founded about
fifty years later.   South Carolina was founded in 1669,
by Governor Sayle; Pennsylvania in 1682, by Wm.
Penn, and other members of the Society of Friends;
North Carolina, about the year 1728; Georgia, in

1732; Kentucky, in 1773; Vermont, about 1764, by emigrants from Connecticut and other parts of New England. The states of New England are six in number. Connecticut, Rhode Island, Massachusetts, Vermont, New Hampshire, Maine. The union now consists of twenty-six states.

Our commerce and navigation were soon greatly benefited by these noble colonies; and by their rapid growth and prosperity they were adding continually to the strength and resources of the empire. At that auspicious period of their common history, the government of the mother country attempted to tax the colonies without the intervention of their local legislatures, on the ground of sovereignty alone —a sovereignty exercised by the British crown and by the parliament in which the people of those remote settlements were not represented by a single member chosen by themselves. The obnoxious laws which the Americans resolved to resist as tyrannical, were a stamp act, a tea tax, a bill for closing the port of Boston, another for altering the constitution of Massachusetts, and a third for removing if necessary the trial of capital offenders to Great Britain. These unwise measures were at first popular in England; and it was a common opinion that the Americans, on the pretext of seeking a redress of grievances, contemplated absolute independence. The Americans, on the other hand, too hastily concluded that the arbitrary acts of the government were the commencement of a system of tyranny. Both views were erroneous. If the wise counsels of Lord Chatham and Mr. Burke, so strenuously urged by them with powerful reasoning and energetic eloquence, had prevailed at an early period of the dispute, the breach might have been healed. But the concessions of the British cabinet all came too late, were in themselves insufficient, and consequently they were unavailing. The vicious principle of taxing the unrepresented colonies was never conceded. In 1775 civil war began at Lexington. Yet even then, if the Americans had been promptly restored to their rights as British subjects, a final separation might have been avoided. But the unwise endeavour to compel three millions of freemen of British origin to submit to injustice, by subduing the American continent, was persisted in, and in July, 1776, they declared their independence. For more than a century they had grown up under the fostering wing of the parent state, whose mistaken policy, during two years, was the means of casting them off for ever.

It might have been too flattering to our pride and ambition to retain the sovereignty of the best portion of the New World in addition to the other vast and important dominions of the British crown. And by the American declaration of independence that high trust, that growing power and responsibility, and that immense empire, were wrested from England.* At the distance of sixty-six years we can better estimate the magnitude of the loss.

Henceforth each nation must pursue its separate career: but their language and literature are one; many British emigrants are annually added to the number of American citizens, and not less than thirty thousand British seamen man the vessels of the United States. With so many ties of kindred, of liberty, of language, of literature, of commerce, and of religion, to bind us in unity and concord, it were deplorable indeed, if the recollection of ancient grievances, if more recent and

---

* Mr. Webster, in his speech at Boston, in September, 1842, said, "In case of a war between England and the United States, the only eminent advantage with either party would be found in the rectitude of her cause. With right on our side we are a match for England—with right on her side she is a match for us or any nation." That opinion was warranted by history.

more trivial differences, if low, unkind, and ungenerous prejudices should perpetuate former alienation and antipathy. The star of peace is now in the ascendant—may it herald the dawn of a happier day. Long may both nations continue in friendly relationship. Strong in their amity, England and America might consecrate and combine their energies to prevent tyranny and war, and might pursue together the glorious career of civilization, dispensing the highest blessings to mankind in both hemispheres.

The political system of the United States was formed by recasting the institutions of our common ancestors in a republican mould. It is proposed to consider the American constitution by comparing it, in the most essential points, with that of Great Britain, as the most interesting and instructive light in which it can be viewed by Englishmen.

The Americans generally evince an almost exclusive partiality for their country and its institutions; and an Englishman may, with equal reason be allowed to regard Great Britain and its constitution with preference and attachment. It is perhaps scarcely possible for either an American or an Englishman, who loves his country, to view the institutions of both nations from a strictly neutral position. It is not however the object of the following enquiry to draw a comparison, either flattering or adverse to the one or to the other great nation. I have endeavoured, at least, to treat the subject with impartiality.

In preparing these papers, I have chiefly had recourse to the well-known French work, "De la Democratie en Amerique," by M. De Tocqueville,* the most

---

* A few of the quotations are taken from Mr. Reeves's excellent translation, which I did not meet with until after having read the original work.

able, complete, and candid treatise on the government of the United States. The author is of republican opinions, and he has said, "that having been bred in the midst of revolutions and counter-revolutions, despotisms, restorations, and all the miseries of insecurity, political and personal, he was the better able to view the worst that passes in America with calmness."— *Quarterly Review*, No. 113.

I have dispensed with the aid which might perhaps have been derived from the narratives of several clever and amusing travellers, whose opinions some at least might have been disposed to call in question, as prejudiced against the United States, preferring the testimony of such as have visited America with impressions favourable to its democratic institutions. The works of respectable English travellers are of course good evidence of matters of fact coming under their own observation.

Some untravelled Englishmen, judging of other countries by flattering report, and of their own by sober experience, and having had to encounter the ills that are common to humanity, and which necessarily exist, (especially during periods of distress) in our own populous commercial nation, are desirous that England should be transformed into something very different from what she has been heretofore. They do not deny that we have rather more liberty than the Russians, the Turks, or the Chinese; but the measure of freedom we enjoy as the happy result of the monarchical, aristocratic, and popular principles, which are duly tempered and harmoniously blended in the British constitution, does not satisfy them. They long for the *purer* liberty of a pure democracy; and the country from which they draw their favourite arguments and most persuasive illustrations, is the United States of America.

That republican America has hitherto greatly prospered cannot be denied.  But because democracy and prosperity have coexisted in the United States, it does not necessarily follow that democracy was either the sole or the principal cause of that prosperity;—far less does it follow that democracy would be the cause of greater prosperity to England, than she enjoys under her limited monarchy.  There are politicians who have but one theory for all circumstances, and who would have all nations to adopt their favourite form of government.  But government is a science eminently practical, and it were a most unreasonable opinion that, because the constitution of the United States may be suitable for them, it must also be proper for England,—the circumstances of the two countries being widely different.

America is far separated by her geographical position from the kingdoms of Europe, and rarely need she involve herself in European alliances or hostilities.  Contented with her own immense resources, she may prosper, undisturbed by the troubles and the conflicts which agitate the old world.  As regards foreign powers, a neutral and defensive attitude is the natural and wise policy which was recommended to her by the great Washington, and which her best statesmen have endeavoured to maintain.  That admirable man, in his farewell address to his countrymen on retiring from public life, exhorted them to be impartial and neutral with respect to the nations of Europe, to have as little connexion as possible with them.  "Why," says he, "entangle our peace and prosperity in the toils of European ambition, rivalship, interest, humour, or caprice?"  If the Americans ever again involve themselves in European warfare, it will be in spite of a geographical position the most favourable to peace.  The immense extent of their cultivated and uncultivated territory is not less conducive to internal tranquillity.

Numbers of native Americans, with a spirit of restless
enterprise, are continually forming new settlements in
the wilderness, and clearing away the forest where the
savage lately pursued his game.   The first cultivators
reap the rich produce of a virgin soil, probably soon
leave their farms to others, and penetrate yet farther
into the desert in quest of new possessions.   At the
first approach of civilized man, the herds of wild ani-
mals, on which the Indians subsist, retire into deeper
solitudes, and their Indian hunters must follow them.
They part with a portion of their territory to the federal
government, or to one of the states, for an almost
nominal price.   The land speculators occupy it, and
thus the boundary of civilization is constantly encroaching on that of savage life.   The power of these savages
has been broken by the wars in which they have been
provoked to engage, and which have generally termi-
nated in their extirpation or banishment to a more
distant part of the great forest.   Their deserted territory is then added to the United States.   Thus, as the
Indians have said, with melancholy truth, "the red
man melts away like snow, and the white man's for
ever does not last long enough."*   In proportion to its

* "There chanced to be on board this boat, in addition to
the usual dreary crowd of passengers, one Pitchlynn, a chief
of the Choctaw tribe of Indians, who *sent in his card* to me,
and with whom I had the pleasure of a long conversation.
. . . . . . . . . . He was dressed in our ordinary
every-day costume, which hung about his fine figure loosely,
and with indifferent grace.   On my telling him that I re-
gretted not to see him in his own attire, he threw up his
right arm for a moment, as though he were brandishing
some heavy weapon, and answered, as he let it fall again,
that his race were losing many things beside their dress, and
would soon be seen upon the earth no more; but he wore it
at home, he added, proudly.
" He told me that he had been away from his home, west

population, no other country has so great resources and so extensive a territory as America. It has a moveable frontier of indefinite extent. In Massachusetts, the most populous part of the union, the number of inhabitants in 1837 was only eighty-four to a square mile, or not one third of the general rate of population throughout England and Wales. In other parts of the United States the population is far more widely scattered. It has increased however with wonderful rapidity. In the year 1643, the number of settlers in New England was twenty-one thousand two hundred : a century afterwards they had increased to half a million; and now, at the distance of two centuries, the population of the United States is seventeen millions, and of late has doubled itself in about twenty-five years.

The English law of inheritance, which gives the paternal estate to the eldest son, was soon set aside in the United States. When an American dies without a will, his property goes to his heirs in a direct line. If there are several heirs of the same degree, they inherit equally. If there is one only, that heir or heiress succeeds to the whole. In the state of Vermont the male

---

of the Mississippi, seventeen months : and was now returning. He had been chiefly at Washington on some negociations pending between his tribe and the government: which were not settled yet (he said in a melancholy way), and he feared never would be : for what could a few poor Indians do against such well-skilled men of business as the whites ? . . . . . . . . . . . . There were but twenty thousand of the Choctaws left, he said, and their number was decreasing every day. A few of his brother chiefs had been obliged to become civilised, and to make themselves acquainted with what the whites knew, for it was their only chance of existence. But they were not many; and the rest were as they always had been. He dwelt on this, and said several times that unless they tried to assimilate themselves to their conquerors, they must be swept away before the strides of civilised society."—DICKENS's *American Notes.*

heir is entitled to a double portion. But an American has full power to dispose of his property by will as he pleases, and most of the states allow entails under certain restrictions.

The destination of estates to a *long series* of heirs by strict entail, as in Scotland, is an unnatural and undue restraint unfavourable to national prosperity. The English system might possibly be improved, but on the whole, the legal and customary transmission of estates from father to son, without minute and perpetual subdivision, works well and in harmony with our institutions. The heir to the estate uses his influence to promote the success of his younger brothers, and all, from family attachment and mutual interests, are generally inclined to aid each other.

The abolition of the law of primogeniture leads to the multiplication of petty landholders. In France the law *obliges* the testator to divide his property among his heirs in equal, or nearly equal, proportions. Now, from Mr. McGregor's valuable Report respecting French Commerce, which has lately been published under the sanction of our Board of Trade, it appears that there are no less than ten millions nine hundred thousand landed proprietors in France, being nearly one third of the whole population. This parcelling out of the soil among a multitude of petty proprietors is a great impediment not only to agricultural but also to commercial improvement, and it is one great cause of the injurious illiberality of the French tariff.

In the United States the evils which result from the excessive subdivision of the land have not yet been seriously felt, for there the law does not *compel* the testator, as in France, to subdivide his property; and land is so easily obtained, that the father's estate generally goes to the eldest son, while the other sons betake themselves to the wilderness.

There is a perpetual stream of emigration from the older states to the unoccupied lands in the west, while of the emigrants newly arrived from Europe, a great number are employed in the older states as labourers. Thus there is plenty of employment. The feeble and infirm may be overlooked and outstripped in the race, but the bold, active, and persevering, who either make or mar the prosperity and peace of a country, can provide for themselves. The people employed in manufactures, and liable to be suddenly reduced to idleness and want by reverses in trade are few. If any are dissatisfied with their lot, they can readily change it. Thus the most frequent causes of discontent and tumult are obviated. Those elements of discord which, in more densely peopled countries, come into angry collision, are harmlessly dissipated in the United States.

M. De Tocqueville met with a French refugee in the wilds of America, who, in his native country, had been a violent republican, and in embarrassed circumstances. During several years of prosperity in his new condition, his opinions were entirely changed. As a prosperous landholder, far removed from the political strife of cities and revolutions, his violent prejudices and animosities had expired, and he had become an advocate for the rights of property and the principles of order and good government, which he formerly endeavoured to subvert.

And here it may be observed, that how propitious soever to the internal tranquillity of America this mode of occupancy may be, it is far less favourable to the proper cultivation of the soil than the English system of landlord and tenant, a contract between two parties, the practical tendency of which is to improve the land to the utmost. In order to obtain a good tenant and a high rent, the landlord must employ his capital in substantial improvements and repairs of the farm ; and by the conditions of his lease he binds the tenant to cultivate it in the best manner. As the tenant is prevented from injuring the land, so he can only make it yield enough to pay the rent and his own profit by diligent, economical, and skilful culture.

Hence the superior husbandry, the fine corn fields, the rich and well stocked pastures, and the comfortable homesteads of our native England. But in America, where land is abundant, and the *owner* is also the *cultivator* of the soil, it frequently happens that he endeavours to make the most of it during the period of his occupancy, and the land is consequently impoverished by waste. If we have not plains of immense extent and natural fertility, and vast primeval forests undisturbed by the axe and the plough, has not the all-bountiful Creator bestowed on our nation blessings of another kind ;—superior skill in arts, manufactures, and agriculture, commerce which brings to our shores the produce of every climate ; and colonies where many of our countrymen have found competency and wealth ? In England there is great inequality of condition, the consequence of a very advanced state of civilization ; and there are sudden changes from great commercial and manufacturing prosperity to adverse times. These are extensively and severely felt by all classes, especially by those dependent on the wages of labour, who are too often as improvident in the day of prosperity, as if adversity would never come. Still, let a fair comparison be made between the condition of the people of England and those of other countries, and it will be found that none of them possess the elements of social happiness in greater measure than our own highly-favoured nation. Above all, we hope to shew that Great Britain is pre-eminently blessed in the enjoyment of true and well regulated freedom, and in the provision made for the religious instruction of the people.

Another important point in which America differs from England is, that she has no great overgrown metropolis like London.

> Here malice, rapine, accident, conspire,
> And now a rabble rages, now a fire;
> Their ambush here relentless ruffians lay,
> And here the fell attorney prowls for prey;
> Here falling houses thunder on your head,
> And here a female atheist talks you dead.
> DR. JOHNSON'S *London.*

When Mr. Jefferson was in Paris during the French Revolution, he remarked, that if his country had a city like the French capital, it would soon be the ruin of her institutions. Yet Paris was the birth place of French republicanism. But it is curious and instructive, that when the self-styled " Friends of the people" in Europe were exulting at the nativity, as they supposed, of universal freedom, so able a man and so fervent a democrat as Jefferson, beheld in those horrid scenes of tumult and slaughter what made him moralize and tremble for the future destiny of republican America, if ever it should contain a great metropolis, where democracy might concentrate its energies, and display its unbridled licentiousness. Jefferson doubtless foresaw that republican anarchy could not last long, and that the tyranny of the many would swiftly resolve itself into the tyranny of one. The reign of terror in Paris was quickly followed by the despotic reign of Napoleon, who had the art of gratifying at once his own ruling passion and that of the French people. *His* victories were *theirs;* he might freely indulge his own pride, vanity, and boundless ambition, so long as the citizens of Paris were delighted with the pomps, shews, and shadows of military glory. His police and soldiers overawed the mob, his conscriptions drew off the fiery youth from the provinces, and his soldiers were ready to die by thousands at the bidding of their victorious general, for the love of fighting, pay, plunder, glory, and licentiousness.

We have considered three very essential points of difference between the condition of America and that of Great Britain. *First*, in consequence of the remoteness of America from Europe she is less liable to be involved in foreign wars, or to be affected by the political convulsions that agitate European society. *Secondly*, she has at present abundant employment for her population, and an ample territory in reserve. And *Thirdly*, she has *not* a great overgrown metropolis like London. These circumstances greatly tend to promote internal tranquillity and to prevent the excesses of democratic violence. From these preliminary considerations it may be inferred, that political institutions under which America has prospered, might nevertheless prove disastrous to England.

The origin and progress of the constitutions of the two countries were also widely different. The republican sentiments of the first colonists had been encouraged and strengthened while the colonies were rising into importance; and the only link which bound them to a monarchy having been finally broken, they were at liberty to frame for themselves a form of government congenial with their original character, their early history, and their existing circumstances. During the war, Washington had painful experience of the evils arising from a feeble executive. The several states of the union were independent republics. Congress could only recommend them to tax themselves, but had no power to raise money for defraying the expenses of the war. The army was ill appointed, often without pay and provisions: Congress had recourse to issues of paper money, which soon became almost valueless. The troops mutinied, and nothing but the high character and influence of their great commander, and their ardent enthusiasm in favour of independence and against England, kept them together till a loan was obtained from France.

The degree in which the popular will should predominate under the new constitution was the subject of much consideration and debate, and gave rise to two great parties. The Federalist party comprehended the ablest and most illustrious Americans, as Washington, Hamilton, Adams, Madison, and Jay, who were convinced of the excellence of the British constitution and of the necessity of a vigorous executive. The ascendancy of the Federalists was of short duration. Washington was elected the first President of the United States in 1789; the next was Adams; and in the year 1800 Jefferson was appointed his successor. Jefferson's election as President at the commencement of the present century may be considered as the æra of the ascendancy of the democratic party, which is now entirely dominant.

The constitution of the United States was prepared by a body of the most eminent citizens, on a great and sudden emergency. But without disparagement to their talents and integrity it may be affirmed, that a government so formed can only be a legislative experiment. That experiment is—with *how little* restraint and controul can a great nation continue to exist in social order and happiness? It has been made under the most favourable circumstances, in a newly discovered continent, remote from disturbing causes; and were it successful, it would *not* be a precedent for European kingdoms. A democratic government has doubtless in many respects been well suited to the *developement* of the resources of America, during its colonization by persons of all nations, conditions, and characters, scattered over its wide domain, dwellers often in solitary independence. But when the waste lands shall be nearly occupied, and the people become crowded together in cities, then the period of trial will come. It is only fifty-three years since Washington was first elected President. The government has since become more and more democratic, and time and events must prove whether it can last.

But the foundation of the British constitution is laid deep, in a monarchy of more than a thousand years' duration. We trace it in the customs of our Saxon ancestors; in their Wittenagemote, or national council, in the wise laws of Alfred, in the charters obtained from our monarchs, in the concessions made by Charles I. to Parliament. It withstood the rude shock of civil war and usurpation. The monarchy was again restored; and at length, in the year 1688, that ever memorable and glorious æra of our history, the government was clearly, solemnly, and wisely defined and settled on the solid and lasting basis of our protestant religion and our ancient liberties.*

Thus the British constitution was not the contrivance of a congress, or assembly of politicians, at any given period. It has grown like the stately oak, to which it has often been compared, firmly rooted in the native soil, where it flourishes with venerable beauty and the strength of years. It has been matured, as the character of a man ripens and improves by education and experience, to wisdom and virtue. It has been perfected by various trials and successes, by the mutual conflicts and concessions of the several estates of the

---

* King William's first declaration stated, "that he had nothing before his eyes in this undertaking, but the preservation of the protestant religion, and the securing to the nation the free enjoyment of their laws, rights, and liberties, under a just and legal government." See also the Bill of Rights.

realm, during which errors and abuses have been corrected, the best checks against tyranny and violence, and the strongest safeguards of liberty have been established. " Our ancestors," as Burke beautifully observes, " by the modesty as well as by the energy of their minds, went on insensibly drawing this constitution nearer and nearer to its perfection, by never departing from its fundamental principles, nor introducing any amendment, which had not a *subsisting root* in the laws, constitution, and usages of the kingdom."

Hence the people of England will not destroy their constitution, until the lofty spirit of their ancestors shall have fled, and their characteristic love of justice, order, and freedom, their respect for religion, morality, and law, shall have disappeared in turbulent folly and base degeneracy. Together have the British character and the British constitution flourished, and together only will they perish.

# PROVINCIAL INSTITUTIONS—OUTLINE OF AMERICAN CONSTITUTION.

## LECTURE II.

Close resemblance between the municipal and provincial institutions of England and America—Outline of the American constitution—The federal government of the United States—If at the æra of the French Revolution and of the new constitution of America, Great Britain had been a republic, could she have preserved her freedom?

On the wise and equitable principle, that concerns in which individuals and communities are immediately interested, are best conducted by themselves, the business of parishes, towns, and cities, is managed in England, in vestries, in petty sessions, in quarter sessions, chosen by and from among the people. From the great public works of our commercial cities, to the repairs of a parish road or sewer,—from the highest to the lowest offences within the range of local jurisdiction, matters relating to the prosperity, convenience, security, health, and morals of particular neighbourhoods, are placed under the direction of individuals and corporate bodies appointed and residing there.

In the United States the same admirable system exists, with variations as to the details, which it would be tedious to mention.

In the smaller towns of the northern states, the inhabitants choose annually " Select men," from three to nine in number, in whom the municipal authority is chiefly vested. They usually act on their own responsibility, carrying out principles previously recognized by the majority. But when any thing unusual is to be done, or if ten citizens demand a town meeting, the select men must summon it. In the smaller towns there are some deviations from this system: the larger ones have a mayor and corporation. Besides the select men, there are nineteen principal officers in a town, annually elected, and most of whom have salaries.

From England the Americans have adopted the office of justice of the peace. They have sessions and also grand juries, commissioners for turnpikes and sewers, and other county and parish officers. In the southern states the power of the local authorities in the towns is more limited, and in the counties it is greater. Between this part of the institutions of England and those of America, there is a near family resemblance.

> " Facies non omnibus una :
> Nec diversa tamen ; qualem decet esse sororum."

In both countries the state leaves the conduct of local affairs to local officers, who are amenable to the courts of law for the neglect or abuse of their authority. These municipal and provincial institutions are strongholds of liberty, and nurseries of patriotic feeling. They are invaluable privileges, whose good effects are manifest in the unfettered activity which prevails in this country.

Even in undertakings of great magnitude, which are rather national than merely local, as railways, the legislature gives full scope to individual enterprize, interfering only for the protection of vested rights and

interests, and for the public advantage. " I have visited,"
says M. De Tocqueville, " the two nations in which the
system of provincial liberty has been most perfectly
established, and I have listened to the opinions of different parties in those countries.   In America I met
with men who secretly aspired to destroy the democratic
institutions of the union; in England I found others
who openly attacked the aristocracy; but I know of no
one who does not regard provincial independence as a
great benefit.   In both countries I have heard a thousand different causes assigned for the evils of the state;
but among these the local system was never mentioned.
I have heard citizens attribute the power and prosperity
of their country to a variety of causes; but they *all*
placed the advantages of local institutions in the foremost rank."

Thus, in common with the Americans, we possess,
beyond all other nations, liberty in those concerns that
come within the range of personal and daily experience.
Where arbitrary interference would most injure our prosperity, where the chains of servitude would gall us the
most,—where liberty, in short, is most essential—there
Englishmen are happily and essentially free.

Each state of the union has a senate and a house of
representatives.   Pennsylvania originally committed
the whole legislative power to one representative body,
a plan which was at first approved by Benjamin Frank-
lin, as more consistent with his favourite dogma of the
people's sovereignty.   Experience soon convinced the
Pennsylvanians of their error, and they were obliged
to follow the example of New England and of Old
England likewise.

The members of both branches of the *state* legislatures are elected in the same manner, and by the same
citizens: the senators, usually for a period of two or
three years, and the representatives for one year only.

The senates are gradually renewed by the annual retirement of a certain number of members, and the election of successors.

By dividing the legislature into two branches, the founders of the constitution did not intend to create an aristocratic body, but by the mutual check of two assemblies to secure greater deliberation, and also to form a court of appeal for the revision of the laws.

The executive power of each state is principally vested in the governor. He apprises the legislature of the wants of the public service, and may suggest the means of providing for them. In general, the governor carries into effect the measures of the legislature, but they sometimes appoint special agents for that purpose. He may suspend their measures by his veto. In the administration of affairs in the counties and towns, he never interferes except to appoint justices of the peace. He has the controul of the military power of the state.

The governor is a magistrate chosen by the people for a term of one or two years, and consequently he is dependent on the majority from whom his short-lived power is derived.

Having thus given a brief general outline of the governments of the states, we proceed to consider the federal or supreme government of the union. The first *federal constitution* was formed in 1778, and was finally adopted by all the states in 1781. At the close of the war with England the several states had virtually become independent, their union was scarcely more than nominal, and was on the eve of dissolution. The task of framing a new and improved constitution was entrusted to an assembly of fifty-five members, among whom were Madison and Hamilton and Washington, the last being President. The new federal government entered upon its functions in 1789, at the commencement of the French Revolution. The powers

vested in the federal government and in the several
states are well explained in the following passage from
the Federalist, a celebrated work written by General
Hamilton, with the exception of a few papers by Jay
and Madison:—"The powers delegated by the constitution of the federal government are few and defined.
Those which are to remain in the state governments
are numerous and indefinite; the former will be exercised principally on external objects, as war, peace,
negociation, and foreign commerce. The powers reserved to the several states will extend to all the objects
which, in the ordinary course of affairs, concern the
internal order and prosperity of the state."—*Federalist*,
No. 45.

The federal government has therefore the sole right
to declare war,—to conclude treaties of peace and of
commerce,—to raise a naval and military force,—to
exercise controul over the finances, and to impose taxes.
It likewise has some other functions in matters which
concern the states generally. It has *two legislative
assemblies*, the *senate* and the *house of representatives*.
If the number of members which each state should
send to Congress had been regulated solely by the
amount of its population, the influence of the smaller
states in Congress would have been overborne; and on
the contrary their influence would have unduly pre-
ponderated, if an equal number of representatives in
*both* houses had been allotted to each state, irrespective
of the amount of its population.

It was finally determined that, to secure the *independence of the states*, each of them should send to
Congress two senators; but in order to maintain the
*sovereignty of the people*, the number of members
which each state should be entitled to send to the
house of representatives should be in proportion to its
population; namely, one member for every thirty

thousand inhabitants. Hence it has come to pass, that while the small state of Delaware sends to the house of representatives only one member, the populous state of New York sends forty members. Congress may raise the numerical standard of inhabitants, who are to return one member to the house of representatives. Virginia and other slave-holding states send members to Congress in proportion to the number of their slaves, as well as of their free citizens, although the slaves themselves have virtually no political privileges. In the *senate* each state is represented by two members only.

It might happen therefore that the minority of the nation should return the majority of senators, and so oppose the decisions of the other house which is elected by the majority of the people. With respect to this anomaly M. De Tocqueville observes, "It is only in the origin of societies that the laws can be completely consistent with theory. When you see a nation en-joying this advantage, do not too hastily conclude that it is wise, but rather remember that it is young." This shews how rare and difficult it is to combine logically and rationally all the parts of a legislative system.

The *house of representatives* is elected by the people, and the term for which the members are chosen is two years.

The members of the *senate* must be thirty years of age, residing in the state they represent, and citizens of nine years' standing. They are elected by the *legislatures of each state* and for a period of six years, one third of their number going out by rotation every second year.

Thus the house of representatives is *directly* chosen by the people; but the senate is appointed by *elected bodies.* No person is eligible as a representative who is not twenty-five years old and resident in the state in

D

which he is chosen, and who has not been a citizen for
seven years.   No qualification in property is required.
The functions of the house of representatives are purely
legislative.   It has also the right of impeaching public
officers.

The senate, besides its legislative powers, has the
right of trying political offences brought before it by
the other chamber.   It is also the great executive
council of the nation.   The treaties concluded by the
President must be ratified by the senate, and his appointments must have their sanction.

The *executive power* of the union is vested in the
President, who is a magistrate chosen for a period of
four years, and is re-eligible.   His power is kept in
check by the people who conferred it, and by the senate
who can annul certain acts of his.   The senate cannot
however compel him to take any measure, nor do they
participate in the exercise of his authority.   The President has a suspensive veto, whereby he is able to
arrest the progress of laws that might abridge his power,
and it obliges the senate to reconsider any measure
to which he thus objects.   The legislature would undoubtedly prevail in any struggle with the President
by persevering in its course;  but the veto renders it
necessary to review the measure, and a majority of two
thirds of the whole house is then requisite before it can
become law.

Two dangers which especially threaten democracies
are, first, *the entire subjection of the legislative bodies
to the will of the electors;* and second, *the absorption
of all the other powers of government by the legislature.*
The federal government is rather less exposed to these
dangers than the state governments, having been formed
subsequently and with greater skill, by the wisest, ablest,
and most patriotic of American statesmen.

" The federal government," says M. De Tocqueville,

" is more just and more moderate than that of the states. Its designs are characterised by greater wisdom, its projects by more consistency and foresight; its measures are executed with greater skill, steadiness, and perseverance.".........." In America the subjects of the union are not states but private citizens. The national government levies a tax, not upon the state of Massachusetts, but upon each of its inhabitants. All former confederate governments presided over communities, but that of the union rules individuals; its force is not borrowed but self-derived, and it is served by its own civil and military officers, by its own army, and its own courts of justice. It cannot be doubted that the spirit of the nation, the passions of the multitude, and the provincial prejudices of each state tend to abridge the power of a federal government so constituted, and to facilitate the means of resistance to its authority."

The American union is superior to all other federal governments, being permanent leagues of independent states, submitting, *as states,* to one central authority. The central government of America is partly national and partly federal, exercising authority over all American citizens in matters in which they are generally interested.

*The circumstances under which the American confederacy arose* were unusually favourable. The Anglo-American colonies, speaking one language, as nearly resembling each other in manners, customs, laws, civilization, as the inhabitants of different counties and provinces in a European kingdom, were separated from the mother country, and they united together under one government, so as to combine the superior happiness and freedom of small republics with the power of a great nation.

Nevertheless the inherent defect of a confederacy is its weakness, and the stability of the American union, hitherto, is in a great measure owing to geographical position, extent of territory, and other peculiar advantages already adverted to, which favour its internal tranquillity and its peace with foreign nations.

A federal system is necessarily complex, as involving two sovereignties which are liable to come into collision.

"In examining the constitution of the United States," says M. De Tocqueville, "which is the most perfect federal constitution that ever existed, one is amazed at the variety of information and the excellence of discretion which it presupposes in the people it is meant to govern."—"When once the general theory is comprehended, numberless difficulties remain to be solved in its application; for the sovereignty of the union is so involved in that of the states, that its boundaries cannot be immediately distinguished. The whole structure of the government is artificial and conventional; and it would be ill adapted to a people that had not been long accustomed to conduct its own affairs; or to one in which the science of politics had not descended to the humblest classes of society."

The attempt to transfer this form of government to Mexico has proved an utter failure.*   It is needless to

---

* "The seductive example, then always growing in the United States of America, induced us to adopt without discretion its system of government, proper only for that singular people, who, in times more recent, have begun to fall into confusion, and to give way to the complication and debility of its institutions. Transcendant was the error of imagining that the United States were indebted for their prosperity to the institutions, and not to the character of the people. We conceived that by writing down for ourselves the same laws, and adopting the same codes, we might effect a complete revolution in the habits, in the customs, and in the genius of the nation. ...... Deeply engaged in imitating the great model, copies of sovereignty were formed,

observe that a confederacy of republics would be quite inapplicable to the British empire; and there is no example in history of a great nation which has long existed as a *consolidated* republic.—"All the passions," says De Tocqueville, " fatal to republics increase with the extent of territory, whilst the virtues which tend to their preservation do not proportionably increase."

But even in America the weakness of the central government relatively to that of the particular states is a serious defect.

In the year 1801, on the occasion of the election of the President, the requisite majority could not be obtained in favour of any individual, and four days of balloting did not produce a single change of vote. The party opposed to Mr. Jefferson then proposed "to pass a law for putting the government into the hands of an officer." But Mr. Jefferson himself informs us, in his Memoirs, (vol. III. p. 460,) " We thought it best to declare openly and firmly, one and all, that the day such an act passed the middle states *would arm,* and that no such usurpation, even for a single day, should be submitted to."

In the war of 1812, the President ordered the militia to proceed towards the frontiers. The states of Connecticut and Massachusetts refused on several pretexts to furnish their contingent, and persisted in that refusal in spite of the mandate of the federal government.

The doctrine of " nullification," as it is called, is

with all the apparatus of independent states, the which augmented the divisions and the sacrifices of the people. All was weakness and disunion, because in the federal system the action of the government is almost null. But why dilate on the enumeration of facts and circumstances with which every one is conversant?"—*Speech of* SANTA ANNA, *Provisional President of the Mexican Republic, on the opening of the session of Congress,* 10*th of June,* 1842.

advocated by Mr. Calhoun, one of the ablest speakers in the American senate, and by other statesmen, and it has been maintained by South Carolina and some other states. The purport of that doctrine is, that a single state assumes to itself the right of abrogating or annulling, within its own limits, a law which has been passed by the constitutional representatives of the whole twenty-six states of the union assembled in Congress.

There has been a recent revolutionary attempt in Maryland, to subvert the existing government, and to set up a new one.

There was lately a serious convulsion in Rhode Island, which having been briefly described by the celebrated American orator, Mr. Clay, in a speech delivered at Lexington, Kentucky, in 1842, I shall quote his own words :—

"That little, but gallant and patriotic state, had a charter, derived from a British king, in operation between one and two hundred years. There had been engrafted upon it laws and usages from time to time; and altogether a practical constitution sprung up, which carried the state, as one of the glorious thirteen, through the revolution, and brought her safely into the union. Under it, her Greens and Perrys, and other distinguished men, were born and rose to eminence. The legislature had called a convention to *remedy whatever defects it had, and to adapt it to the progressive improvements of the age.* In that work of reform, the Dorr party might have co-operated ; but, *not choosing so to co-operate, and in wanton defiance of all established authority,* they undertook subsequently to call another convention. The result was two constitutions, not *essentially differing* on the principal point of controversy, the right of suffrage.

"The Dorr party proceeded to put their constitution in operation, by electing *him* as the governor of the state, members to the mock legislature, and other officers. But they did not stop here; they proceeded to collect, to drill, and to marshal a military force, and pointed their cannon against the arsenal of the state.

" The President was called upon to interpose the power of the union, to preserve the peace of the state, in conformity with an express provision of the federal constitution. The leading presses of the democratic party at Washington, Albany, New York, and Richmond, and elsewhere, came out in support of the Dorr party, encouraging them in their work of rebellion and treason. And when matters had got to a crisis, and the two parties were preparing for a civil war, and every hour it was expected to blaze out, a great Tammany meeting was held in the city of New York, headed by the leading men of the party, with a perfect knowledge that the military power of the union was to be employed, if necessary, to suppress the insurrection, and, notwithstanding, they passed resolutions *tending to awe the President, and to countenance and cheer the treason.*"

In the same speech, Mr. Clay also mentions " the refusal of a minority in the legislature of Tennessee to co-operate with the majority, (their constitution requiring the presence of two-thirds of the members,) to execute a positive injunction of the constitution of the United States to appoint two United States senators. In principle, that refusal was equivalent to announcing the willingness of that minority to dissolve the union. For if thirteen or fourteen of the twenty-six states were to refuse altogether to elect senators, *a dissolution of the union would be the consequence.* That minority, *for weeks together, and time after time,* deliberately refused to enter upon the election. And if the union is not *in fact dissolved,* it is not because the principle involved would not lead to a dissolution, but because twelve or thirteen other states have not, like themselves, refused to perform a high constitutional duty. And why did they refuse? *Simply because they apprehended the election to the senate of political opponents.* The seats of the two Tennessee senators in the United States senate are now vacant, and *Tennessee has no voice in that branch of Congress in the general legislation.*"

The serious financial difficulties with which Washington had to contend, during the war with this country, have already been referred to. Not many years since, the credit of the United States stood very high, and their stocks were a favourite investment for the capitalists of Europe. Now they have an empty exchequer, several of the states are unable to pay their dividends to the public creditor, the legislatures of others have proposed to " repudiate" the debts contracted by their predecessors in office, the public securities of the union are in universal discredit, and its currency and finances are in great disorder. Yet the natural resources of the country are great, and the people are most enterprising and energetic.*

* Doubtless the doctrine of repudiation, which has been countenanced by headstrong men of inferior principle, in some of the state legislatures, would be utterly rejected by Congress, and by all respectable and honourable Americans. Mr. Webster, in a speech delivered at Boston, on the 30th of September, 1842, said :—" We have national stock which ought to command one hundred and twenty-five per cent. Can a dollar of it be sold ? And this commonwealth, is not even she embarrassed in her operations, and made to feel the blighting influence of a degraded public credit ? And is nobody to make any movement ? Is there no mind large enough, comprehensive enough, to show that it can quit party contest, and devote itself to rebuilding our national credit—to the re-establishment of national faith, and, I may say, character for honour and morals? Some are indiscreet enough to talk of repudiation. Does repudiation cancel a debt ? Is a state not always bound by her debts, notwith-

These are palpable instances of democratic violence and caprice—of the instability and weakness of the federal government. It may continue to exist, while the interests of the different states essentially harmonize with each other, and so long as they are enabled to avoid long and expensive wars. But if circumstances should arise to produce a collision between the states, and if one or more of them should determine to prosecute their own plans and interests in opposition to the rest, it may be inferred from what has formerly happened, that the central government would be unable to controul them, and to prevent a virtual or actual dissolution of the union. That result, in M. De Tocqueville's opinion, would very probably occur, in the event of a protracted war. "The United States," he observes, "are singularly happy, *not* in having a federal constitution which enables them to carry on great wars, but in a geographical position which renders war improbable." And after admiring the enviable lot of nations that can avail themselves of the advantages of a federal government, he adds:—" I do not believe,

standing a declaration that she repudiates them? No, gentlemen, repudiation can do nothing but add disrepute to an acknowledgment of inability to pay. It is our duty to arouse the public mind to this subject. People say that the Europeans ought to make a distinction between the states and the general government. Very true—so they ought; but what then? Are not they all emanations from the same source? And if the states repudiate, may not a European well ask, how long before the general government, the work of the same hands, will do so likewise? Fellow-citizens, this is a stain which we ought to feel more than a wound, and the time has come for the people to address themselves soberly and seriously to the removal of the disgrace. If the doctrine preached in Congress be true, that the public lands are the property of the states—then we have a spot of beginning, then we have a chance by law to induce the states to save their credit and honour."

however, that a union of states could maintain a long contest with a nation of similar resourees, whose government ruled with concentrated authority. A nation which in the presence of *the great military monarchies of Europe* should subdivide its sovereignty, would in my opinion by that very act abdicate its power, and perhaps its existence and its name."

The Americans, like all free nations, are capable of very great warlike efforts, of which they gave proof during their struggle for independence. But a democracy is ill adapted to sustain such exertions with constancy, and for a length of time. The sovereign people are most reluctant to impose upon themselves the heavy burdens and severe privations of protracted warfare. "The relative weakness of democracies in critical periods," observes M. De Tocqueville, "is perhaps the greatest obstacle to the establishment of a republic in Europe. It could only hope to preserve its independence, by the surrounding states becoming democratic likewise. If a republic could prolong its existence for a century, it would probably become at last more wealthy, more populous, and more prosperous than the neighbouring kingdoms; but (and here the monosyllable is all-important) but it would be in danger all the while of being subdued by them." In short, when this fair and flourishing young republic had grown to a proper size and condition, the French or the Russian eagle would probably seize and devour the tempting prey.

If since the American constitution was remodelled and re-established in the year 1789, Great Britain had been a republic, how different *now* might have been her condition, and also the destiny of the other nations of Europe. When we review the history of that eventful period, and trace the desolating course of the French armies, under the reign of the Jacobins and the military tyranny of Napoleon Buonaparte, through Italy, Germany, Spain, and Portugal, to the banks of the Nile, and to burning Moscow; when we remember the strenuous efforts of that ambitious conqueror to destroy British commerce, and to plant his standard on the shores of this island, sacred to liberty, and long unpolluted by the feet of hostile armies; when we recollect how that invader, thirsting for universal dominion, trampled upon the rights of sovereigns and subjects, and disposed of crowns and sceptres at will; and when we turn again to behold our country collected, enduring, undaunted, while nations sank around her, exhausted, in the bloody fray—till at length she drove the tyrant's host from Spain, and with victory on her helm, led the embattled ranks of freedom to the gates of Paris; when we see her once more, defeating the imperial armies, and their chief returned from exile; hurling him from an usurped throne, and securing glorious and lasting peace for the world, at Waterloo;— after reviewing these so memorable events, who can doubt, that if the characteristic fickleness and insubordination of democracy had then divided the councils and enfeebled the energies of our country, Great Britain would have become a French province, and Europe would have been enslaved.

A gracious Providence has clothed this highly favoured nation with the complete armour of a constitution, which combines the greatest freedom of the subject with the utmost energy in the executive government; which gives full scope to the indomitable spirit of a free people, and wields the concentrated power of a mighty monarchy. Thus liberty and right have triumphed, under the British banner; and if ever we surrender that constitution, at faction's bidding, we shall throw away the ample shield of our defence, and yield the glorious ensign under which our fathers conquered.

# ELECTIVE FRANCHISE—LEGISLATIVE ASSEMBLIES.

---

## LECTURE III.

Instability of laws in America—Equality—The ballot—Universal suffrage—Pledged delegates and free representatives—House of Representatives—House of Commons—Senate—House of Lords.

For the important function of making laws, the British constitution aims to employ the collective wisdom and authority of the state, under such checks and safeguards as are admirably calculated to prevent rash and arbitrary legislation. Every law must receive the independent approbation and assent of the house of commons, of the house of lords, and of the sovereign. It must be introduced into both houses of parliament with due notice; the bill must be read a first, a second, and a third time, in both houses; subject to debate, amendment, or rejection, at any stage of its progress. The art of man has not contrived any thing superior to this system, for the preservation of just prerogative and genuine liberty, and the enactment of wise and salutary measures.

The important business of legislation requires to be conducted deliberately, dispassionately, with knowledge, wisdom, and talent; and that would be impossible in promiscuous and irresponsible assemblies of the people. Hence the necessity for the representative system, an improvement so manifest and so generally acknowledged in modern times, that it has been adopted even in democratic states.

The character of the representative assembly must depend in a great measure on the period for which the members are elected, and on the manner of their election.

In this country the parliament is generally dissolved shortly before the expiry of the statutory period of seven years. Of late, owing to the frequent changes of ministry and other causes, the actual duration of parliaments has been much abridged.

According to the theory of the constitution, the members of the house of commons are the *representatives* of the various *classes* of the community. The duration of parliament is such as to enable them to become conversant with public affairs, and accustomed to the forms and business of the house. They enjoy perfect liberty of speech, and are entitled to give an honest vote, after debate and according to their *own judgment.*

In these respects they are distinguished from mere deputies or *delegates* influenced by popular passions and prejudices, and pledged beforehand to vote as certain *electors have dictated.*

The nature and extent of the elective franchise, and the manner of voting for members of parliament in this country, are too well known to require explanation.

In the United States the houses of representatives of the several states and of Congress are chosen annually or biennially, and for the most part by universal suffrage and by ballot. Let us consider the effect of this system in America.

M. De Tocqueville has observed that owing to the

frequency of elections, society in America is kept in a continual state of excitement and agitation, and that there is a great want of system and of stability in the laws.

General Hamilton remarks,* "The facility and the excess of law-making seem to be the diseases to which our governments are most liable. ......The mischievous effects of the mutability in the public councils arising from a rapid succession of new members would fill a volume. Every new election in the states is found to change *one half of the representatives.* From this change of men must proceed a change of opinions and of measures, which forfeits the respect and confidence of other nations, poisons the blessings of liberty itself, and diminishes the attachment and reverence of the people towards a political system which betrays so many marks of infirmity."

Mr. Madison expresses the same sentiment; and Jefferson, in a letter to Madison in 1787, wrote as follows:—" The instability of our laws is really a very serious inconvenience. I think that we ought to have obviated it by deciding that a whole year should always be allowed to elapse between the bringing in a bill, and the final passing of it," &c.

During the last thirty years most of the states have altered their constitutions. Their statute books are exceedingly voluminous. The new statesmen are chiefly desirous to do something, during their term of office, which shall please their constituents; but what their predecessors may have done, they have but little time or inclination to consider. The laws must be without system, and often inconsistent and contradictory, where the authority of the legislator is only a transient emanation from the popular will.

For, lo! push'd up to power, and crown'd their cares,
In comes another set and kicketh them down stairs.

* No. 73 of the Federalist.

The electoral body consists of nearly the whole mass of American citizens, for in most of the states of the union every male citizen of twenty-one years of age has a vote. In several of the states of the union some property qualification is required. In New Jersey, fifty pounds a year; in South Carolina and Maryland, fifty acres of land; in several states, service in the militia or payment of taxes is the qualification; in others, the privilege of voting does not depend on the property of the elector. But in that rising country the possession of some property is so general, that property and the elective franchise are almost co-extensive, for which cause, and for other reasons, the wide diffusion of the franchise is far less perilous than it would be under different circumstances elsewhere.

The very object of elections ought to be *the choice of able and upright statesmen,* well qualified by their character and talents to manage public affairs. Is this end attained by universal suffrage? What says M. De Tocqueville, a competent and impartial witness? " It invariably happens that, in the United States in the present day, the ablest men are *seldom* called to public stations; and it must be acknowledged that this has been the case in proportion as democracy has overstepped its former limits," (which by the way democracy is very apt to do.) " The race of American statesmen has obviously become very degenerate during the last half century."

In endeavouring to account for this fact, M. De Tocqueville remarks on the difficulty of forming a just estimate of the character and qualifications proper for a high and important trust. " Men of superior minds," he says, " may be mistaken; and can it be supposed the multitude will judge more wisely? On the contrary, the opinion of the people is usually formed on a superficial view of the question which they have to consider, and they are attracted by what is shewy and striking, rather than by what is solid and valuable. Hence Charlatans succeed best in pleasing the multitude, whilst those who *really* have the public welfare *at heart* fail to obtain the suffrages of the people."

"Democratic institutions inflame and flatter the passion for equality which they can never satisfy, for the *entire equality* which the people pursue eludes their grasp and mocks them with a perpetual flight."

> That, like the circle, bounding earth and skies,
> Allures from far, yet as they follow flies.

Undoubtedly it does, for although both in the old and the new world demagogues employ the doctrine of equality to delude the people, it is every where the same unreal phantom, alluring only to mislead, disappoint, or destroy.

Thus the writer of an article in the North American Review, (published at Boston in 1831) who is evidently a staunch republican, admits the *fact* of the inequality of conditions even in America, and labours to prove "that there is no necessary or natural connection between the existence of an army of paupers, and incompatibility with republican institutions." As to the fact, however, he says that in Boston there are at least two thousand persons "who get their living by daily begging and fraud. These must be persons of desperate fortune and of abject poverty. There is in the same city a very wealthy class, and between the two extremes there is every intermediate degree." The North American Reviewer further observes, that "the utopian equality of condition, assumed to be necessary to a republic, does not exist in *town* or *country* in the United States." Utopian equality! We thank this candid republican for that word, and would recommend it to the consideration of all who have been accustomed to receive from the lips of demagogues the flattering dogma of the universal equality of mankind. Whereas, on the high authority of M. De Tocqueville and of the Boston reviewer, it appears that the proposition, amended and correctly stated, should stand thus : "*All men are equal*—IN UTOPIA."

Order is heaven's first law; and this confest,
Some are and must be *greater* than the rest,
More rich, more wise; but who infers from hence
That such are *happier*, shocks all common sense.

The Hon. Charles Augustus Murray, a recent and very impartial traveller in the United States, also informs us that the distinctions of rank and station are now as much observed in Philadelphia and Boston as they are in London, or perhaps more so, "only with this difference, that being as it were illegal and unsanctioned by public opinion, they are adhered to with secret pertinacity, and owe their origin and strength principally to wealth;" and the only semblance of republican equality, he tells us, exists among the half civilized settlers in the western wilderness. And M. De Tocqueville says, that while the laws which encourage the division of property have entirely done away with hereditary ranks and distinctions, he knows no country where the love of money has a stronger hold on men's affections, and where greater contempt is expressed for the theory of the permanent equality of property.

As a consequence of that craving insatiable desire for equality, which M. De Tocqueville calls a "democratic instinct," he says the subordinate ranks of society strive to exclude those of superior fortune, talents, and acquirements, from the management of public affairs.

"The people do not view the upper classes with hostile feelings, but they have no good will towards them, and they carefully exclude them from power;

E

superior talents are not the objects of their dread, but
rather of their aversion.   Whoever rises to distinction
without the aid of the people will not be popular."
" On the other hand distinguished men are led to avoid
a career which they cannot pursue independently, and
without demeaning themselves."   He then quotes from
the American work of Chancellor Kent, published in
1830, the following sentiment:—" It is indeed probable
that the men who are best qualified to discharge high
official duties have too much reserve in their manners,
and too much austerity in their principles, for them to
be returned by the majority at an election where universal suffrage is adopted."

M. De Tocqueville sums up his valuable remarks
on this point as follows:—" I hold it to be clear that
those who consider universal suffrage to be a guarantee
of a wise and good choice, labour under a *complete
delusion*.  Whatever may be its advantages, this is not
one of them."

In America *voting by ballot* has been generally
adopted, but in some of the states it has been abandoned
for open voting.   In other states it is still practised.

In this country the votes and proceedings in parliament and at the hustings are all given openly.  Such is
the old constitutional plan, and it is most consistent
with old English honesty and independence.

A party in the state have endeavoured, both in parliament and elsewhere, to engraft on our institutions
secret voting, which would be the first step to the introduction of the democratic electoral system of vote
by ballot, annual parliaments, and universal suffrage.

In clubs and associations, which are a kind of social
partnership, vote by ballot is used with advantage ; for
it enables the members, in the least obnoxious manner,
to exclude those who might disturb the harmony and
defeat the objects of their society.

But there is no analogy whatever between the admission of new members into a club, and the election of representatives to serve in parliament. The elector, by his vote, does not admit the parliamentary candidate into a *private* club or association with *himself*, but in the exercise of an important *public* trust is instrumental in raising him to the office and the responsibility of a legislator. Every speech, every vote in parliament, is known to the nation. Why then should the member be kept in the dark respecting his constituents, their principles, and their opinions? The object of the ballot is to enable the electors to exercise *their* public trust privately and by stealth, while their representative must speak, act, and vote openly. Men wear a mask and hide themselves, not when going to discharge public duties, but to commit secret crimes. If however electors honestly think that any particular candidate deserves their support, what reason have they to be ashamed and afraid of what they do?

" If a man is sheltered from intimidation," says that clever and amusing writer, the Rev. Sydney Smith, " is it at all clear that he would vote from any better motive than intimidation? If you make so tremendous an experiment, are you sure of attaining your object? The landlord has perhaps said a cross word to the tenant; the candidate for whom the tenant votes in opposition to his landlord has taken his second son for a footman, or his father knew the candidate's grandfather: how many thousand votes, sheltered (as the ballotists suppose) from intimidation, would be given from such silly motives as these? how many would be given from the mere discontent of inferiority? or from that strange simious schoolboy passion of giving pain to others, even when the author cannot be found out? —motives as pernicious as any which could proceed from intimidation. So that all voters screened by ballot would not be screened for any public good.

"The Radicals, (I do not use this word in any
offensive sense, for I know many honest and excellent
men of this way of thinking,)—but the Radicals praise
and admit the lawful influence of wealth and power.
They are quite satisfied if a rich man of popular manners gains the votes and affections of his dependents;
but why is not this as bad as intimidation? The real
object is to vote for the good politician, not for the
kind-hearted or agreeable man: the mischief is just
the same to the country whether I am smiled into a corrupt choice, or frowned into a corrupt choice,—what is
it to me whether my landlord is the best of landlords,
or the most agreeable of men? I must vote for Joseph
Hume, if I think Joseph more honest than the Marquis.
The more mitigated Radical may pass over this, but
the real carnivorous variety of the animal should de-
claim as loudly against the fascinations as against the
threats of the great. The man who possesses the land
should never speak to the man who tills it. The intercourse between landlord and tenant should be as
strictly guarded as that of the sexes in Turkey. A
funded duenna should be placed over every landed
grandee.—And then intimidation! Is intimidation
confined to the aristocracy? Can any thing be more
scandalous and atrocious than the intimidation of mobs?
Did not the mob of Bristol occasion more ruin, wretch-
edness, death, and alarm, than all the ejection of tenants,
and combinations against shopkeepers, from the beginning of the century? and did not the Scotch philoso-
phers tear off the clothes of the Tories in Mintoshire?
or at least such clothes as the customs of the country
admit of being worn?—and did not they, without any
reflection at all upon the customs of the country, wash
the Tory voters in the river?

"Some sanguine advocates of the ballot contend
that it would put an end to all canvassing: why should

it do so ?   Under the ballot, I canvass (it is true) a
person who may secretly deceive me.   I cannot be
sure he will not do so—but I am sure it is much less
likely he will vote against me, when I have paid him
all the deference and attention which a representative
bestows on his constituents, than if I had totally neglected him : to any other objections he may have
against me, at least I will not add that of personal
incivility.

"Scarcely is any great virtue practised without some
sacrifice; and the admiration which virtue excites seems
to proceed from the contemplation of such sufferings,
and of the exertions by which they are endured: a
tradesman suffers some loss of trade by voting for his
country; is he not to vote? he might suffer some loss
of blood in fighting for his country; is he not to fight?
Every one would be a good Samaritan, if he was quite
sure his compassion would cost him nothing.   We
should all be heroes, if it were not for blood and frac-
tures; all saints, if it were not for the restrictions and
privations of sanctity; all patriots, if it were not for
the losses and misrepresentations to which patriotism
exposes us.   The ballotists are a set of Englishmen
glowing with the love of England and the love of virtue,
but determined to hazard the most dangerous experiments in politics, rather than run the risk of losing a
penny in defence of their exalted feelings."

Although a few may be willing to hide their heads
with that political timidity which Mr. Sydney Smith
has so well described in the above passage, surely such
is not the *general* wish and feeling of the people of
England.   The ballotists dislike *open* voting, and they
ask for the ballot to shelter themselves from intimidation.   What should we think of a sailor or a soldier
who, because he had a very great dislike to open fighting, should ask leave to hide among the casks in the

ship's hold, or in the bottom of a ditch, by way of shelter from intimidation?

In the army that sort of tremulous aversion to looking the enemy in the face is commonly called "shewing a white feather." Most of us prefer to shew our colours, and to stand by them like men. Britons scorn to skulk from their adversaries, and are accustomed to fight their naval, their military, and why not also their political battles, in open and gallant style. Because some persons consent to lose, in the ballot box, the courageous, manly quality of a free and a brave people, why should those, who are neither ashamed nor afraid, submit to be taken in that trap for the timorous, and there to be curtailed of their national and characteristic honours?

The fox in the fable, who had lost his tail in a trap, cunningly endeavoured to render his own personal defect fashionable, by persuading the rest of his species to part with their brushes likewise. But the wily foxes kept their own wise counsel, and their own handsome tails, and left their brother Reynard alone in his glory.

The ballot, in order to be effectual, must be followed up by a course of double dealing and hypocrisy, which would cast suspicion upon every man's honesty. To quote again from Mr. S. Smith's amusing pamphlet:—" The single lie on the hustings would not suffice; the concealed democrat who voted against his landlord must talk with the wrong people, subscribe to the wrong club, huzza at the wrong dinner, break the wrong head, lead (if he wished to escape from the watchful jealousy of his landlord) a long life of lies between every election; and he must do this, not only *eundo*, in his calm and prudential state, but *redeundo* from the market, warmed with beer and expanded by alcohol; and he must not only carry on his seven years of dissimulation before the world, but in the very bosom of his family, or he must expose himself to the dangerous garrulity of wife, children, and servants, from whose indiscretion every kind of evil report would be carried to the ears of the watchful steward. And when once the ballot is established, mere gentle, quiet lying will not do to hide the tenant who secretly votes against his landlord: the quiet passive liar will be suspected, and he will find, if he does not wave his bonnet and strain his throat in furtherance of his bad faith, and lie loudly, that he has put in a false ball in the dark to very little purpose. Not only you do not protect the tenant who wishes to deceive his landlord, by promising one way and voting another, but you expose all the other tenants, who have no intention of deceiving, to all the evils of mistake and misrepresentation.

" The noise and jollity of a ballot mob must be such as the very devils would look on with delight. A set of deceitful wretches wearing the wrong colours, abusing their friends, pelting the man for whom they voted, drinking their enemies' punch, knocking down persons with whom they entirely agreed, and roaring out eternal duration to principles they abhorred. A scene of wholesale bacchanalian fraud, a *posse comitatus* of liars, which would disgust any man with a free government, and make him sigh for the monocracy of Constantinople."

The ballot is a cover to political fraud. Even in England, where every elector's vote may be known and scrutinized, disgraceful attempts are sometimes made to obtain a majority by personation, double voting, and other nefarious arts. To such evil practices there would be no check whatever, under a system of secret voting.

Such are some of the reasons why the vote by ballot, which is *not acknowledged by the British constitution*, has hitherto been resisted by the leaders both of the Conservative and the Whig parties, as a dangerous

modern innovation. If it were found to answer in
democratic America, it would not by any means follow
that it might be safely and beneficially adopted under
the British monarchy. But if in America the vote by
ballot has failed to secure purity of election; if it has
produced pernicious and bitter fruits even there, he
would be a bold man who should try the experiment
of engrafting on our native institutions that foreign
offshoot of democracy. A single extract from a New
York newspaper, descriptive of the practical influence
of the ballot, as exhibited during the election in 1841,
may tend to deter us from so dangerous a novelty :—

"We begin to fear that this unhappy country is on
the eve of a bloody civil war, a final dismemberment of
the union—the destruction of the present government,
and the ruin of all free institutions. Do you want our
reasons? Here they are. The revelations recently
made, and daily making, of the gross frauds upon the
ballot-box, committed by both parties, give a picture
of demoralization that makes the honest heart sick of
human life. It really appears to us, that whichever
party succeeds at the next election, it will be by fraud
on the ballot-box; and if so, the defeated faction will
not submit, *but resort to physical force to revenge
themselves.* The frauds at Baltimore, the frauds at
Philadelphia, the frauds in Ohio, the frauds in New
York, are revealed and revealing; and in spite of explanations, disclosures, oaths, and affidavits by the
hogshead, we must believe that the political leaders of
both parties are guilty of gross and terrible corruption.
According to the best calculation, it appears that in the
great Atlantic cities, there has been for three years past
a disposable force of five thousand men, distributed in
New York, Philadelphia, Baltimore, Albany, and other
towns, who were put up to the highest bidder, and
driven about from town to town, like cattle, to the poll,

voting as often as they could, and 'laying pipe' in every city and in every ward. Sometimes the Democrats bought up these Hessians—sometimes the Whigs; but they were always to be had by those who had the most money. It appears, also, that this horrible system of fraud had its origin in Philadelphia, and was contemporaneous with the struggles of the United States Bank for a re-charter."

The choice of statesmen in America, and their public conduct, are influenced by several other circumstances, besides the vote by ballot and universal suffrage. By the payment of salaries to representatives and public officers, their appointments become an object of ambition to needy adventurers. The salaries in general are moderate, and in the higher offices are less in proportion than in the subordinate departments. Cheap and dear are relative terms; and an inferior article which is said to cost little, may in fact be dearer than a superior one which costs more. In America the expenses of the government are in the aggregate high, while the character and talents of its functionaries are on the whole of an inferior stamp, and there is a great deal of jobbing and peculation. "I conclude," says M. De Tocqueville, "without having recourse to inaccurate computations, and without hazarding a comparison which might prove to be incorrect, that the democratic government of the Americans is *not* a cheap government; and I predict without hesitation, that if the people of the United States are ever involved in serious difficulties, the rate of taxation will soon be as high as in the greater number of the aristocracies and monarchies of Europe."

In America, as regards either emolument, or continuance in power, or independence in its exercise, there is little to invite or to reward the exertions of distinguished men. Public offices are held on the precarious tenure of the popular favour, and on the

condition of subserviency to the popular will.  Public
men are narrowly and jealously watched; and that
mental superiority which enables a man of talent to
take a more sound and enlarged view of affairs than
the multitude can do, and which renders him their best
representative, is in fact a disqualification for the part
of a mere deputy, who, whatever his own opinions may
be, is to speak and act as those who appoint him may
dictate.   "A proceeding," says M. De Tocqueville,
"which will ultimately set all the securities of representative government at nought, is becoming more and
more general in the United States.   It frequently
happens that the electors in choosing a deputy, pre-
scribe to him a certain line of conduct, and require.
him to pledge himself that he will observe it.   Now,
with the exception of the tumult, this is just the same
as if the majority of the population should hold their
deliberations in the market place."

 · According to the theory and spirit of the British
constitution, such is not the proper position of a member of parliament.   He is not the delegated tool of a
section of the constituency, but the representative of
the whole.   This important principle was admirably
stated by Burke, in his final address to the electors of
Bristol.—" If government were a matter of *will* upon
any side, your's, without question, ought to be superior.
But government and legislation are matters of reason
and judgment, not of inclination.   And what sort of
reason is that, in which the determination precedes the
discussion; in which one set of men deliberate, and
another decide; and where those who form the conclusion are perhaps three hundred miles distant from those
who hear the arguments?   Authoritative instructions,
mandates which the member is bound blindly and implicitly to obey; these are things unknown to the laws
of this land, and which arise from *a fundamental mis-*

*take of the whole order and tenor of our constitution.*
Parliament is not a congress of ambassadors from different states, and with hostile interests, which interests
each must maintain as an agent against other agents;
but parliament is a deliberative assembly of one nation,
with one interest, and that of the whole. You choose
a member indeed; but when you have chosen him, he
is not a member for Bristol, but he is a member of
parliament."

In America, on the contrary, representatives are
more immediately under the controul of their constituents, their dependence upon whom is increased by the
regulation which requires that they shall be inhabitants
of the state they are chosen to represent. In England
a man of talent who may not have " honour in his own
country," is often the successful candidate for some
distant burgh or county, and in the public service he
acquires a national reputation. The American rule
must frequently lead to the choice of men strongly influenced by local and temporary prejudices, but not of
superior ability and worth. It is not surprising, therefore, that able, upright, and independent men, prefer
agriculture, commerce, or a liberal profession, to a
political career, in which they are likely to be outstripped by persons of inferior character and attainments,
but of greater subserviency to the will of the electors.

" I know not," says M. De Tocqueville, " whether
in the United States the people would be willing to
elect men of superior talent, who should ask their
suffrages; but that such men rarely solicit them is
certain." And Mr. Dickens tells us, " that they who
in other countries would, from their intelligence and
station, most aspire to make the laws, do in America
recoil the farthest from that degradation." For these
reasons, and also because the tenure of office of the
representatives, senators, and public functionaries, is

generally too short and uncertain to enable them to acquire experience, the qualifications of American statesmen are seldom of a high order.

Although Pope's well known lines are not absolutely true, they contain truth :—

> For forms of government let fools contest;
> Whate'er is best administered is best.

And it is obvious, that a form of government which from its very nature is administered by inferior and inefficient statesmen cannot be a good one. How far is this view borne out by the character of the legislative assemblies of the United States?

The *house of representatives* of the supreme government at Washington corresponds to the British house of commons. Mr. Fearon, an English radical, thus described it in 1817 :—" They want in appearance the age, experience, dignity, and respectability, which we associate with the idea of legislators, and which are possessed by the superior branch of Congress. ........ Some two or three speakers regularly command attention; others talk on as long as they please, the members being occupied in writing letters, and in reading and folding up newspapers."

M. De Tocqueville, in 1830, described it as follows:—
" When you enter the house of representatives at Washington, you are surprised by the vulgar appearance of that great assembly. In vain do you look around for any man of great celebrity. The members are generally obscure individuals, whose names suggest nothing remarkable. For the most part, they are village attornies, tradesmen, or persons in some humble employment. Though education is almost universal in America, it is said the representatives of the people cannot always write correctly."

The legislative assemblies of some of the states fall

far short even of this standard. For while at the seat of the supreme government, and also in New England, where "Education and liberty are the daughters of morality and religion, and the people are most civilized, democracy makes a better choice than elsewhere; in the more southernly states, on the contrary, talent, education, and virtue in the legislators are more rare; and in the new states (continues the same author) one is amazed to see in what hands power is placed, and is led to wonder by what independent force of legislation and of society the state can prosper."

But even in the federal legislature, three-fourths of the members are lawyers. There is not that variety of professions, and that representation of classes and interests, which characterise the British house of commons.

The following description is from the pen of a still more recent traveller:—"Where sat the many legislators of coarse threats; of words and blows, such as coalheavers deal upon each other, when they forget their breeding? On every side. Every session had its anecdotes of that kind, and the actors were all there. ...... Did I see among them the intelligence and refinement; the true, honest, patriotic heart of America? Here and there were drops of its blood and life, but they scarcely coloured the stream of desperate adventurers, which sets that way for *profit and for pay.*"— DICKENS'S *American Notes.*

America formerly had, and has still, some highly gifted sons. Clay, Webster, Calhoun, Everett, are distinguished names that would do honour to any country. But these gentlemen are all lawyers, and, except the last mentioned, either are or have been senators. It is on the bench, at the bar, in the senate, but not in the house of representatives at Washington, or in other public bodies which are *directly elected by the votes of the great mass of the people,* that the chief

ornaments of their country are to be found; and the
character and proceedings of legislative assemblies must
depend on their general composition rather than on a
few distinguished members.

In this country, at the present moment, specious
but futile arguments regarding what are termed the
*rights* of the people are addressed to them, and are
circulated in cheap publications, far more industriously
and extensively than is generally imagined; and as
antidotes to the poison are not provided with the
same assiduity, it produces much political delusion
and discontent. One of the principal topics of these
appeals is the alleged *right* of the people to universal
suffrage, which is sometimes urged with a solemn
earnestness that would lead one to suppose the deceivers
were themselves deceived by their own false reasoning.
Universal suffrage being treated by them as a right, it is
concluded, of course, that those who have no votes are
" wholly unrepresented." They are said to be " white
slaves,"—" for degradation is degradation still, whatever
may be the outward form of it—it works in the same
way—produces *the same effects.* It matters not whether we affix a stigma by means of the branding iron,
or political exclusion!" According to this kind of
sophistry, the myriads of British subjects in the towns
and counties, who were without votes before the reform
bill, were in as degraded a condition as are the negroes,
now working in gangs in the plantations of Virginia
and the Carolinas!

In his " Reflections on the French Revolution," Mr.
Burke has some admirable remarks on similar specula-
tions concerning the "rights of men," from which I
quote a few sentences, both on account of their excellent wisdom, and to shew that there is no novelty in
the modern fallacies by which the people are now misled. "The pretended rights of these theorists are all

extremes; and in proportion as they are metaphy-
sically true, they are morally and politically false.
The rights of men are in a sort of *middle*, incapable of
definition, but not impossible to be discerned. The
rights of men in governments are their *advantages;*
and these are often in balances between differences of
good; in compromises, sometimes between good and
evil, and sometimes between evil and evil." And again,
"When I hear the simplicity of contrivance aimed at
and boasted of in any new political constitutions, I am
at no loss to decide that the artificers are grossly ignorant of their trade, or totally negligent of their duty.
The simple governments are totally defective, to say
no worse of them."

The *abstract right* of all British subjects to choose
the members of the house of commons being once
admitted, why should the application of the principle
stop there? Why should not the people, as in America, proceed to elect the other branch of the legislature,
and likewise a President instead of their hereditary
monarch? In that small community a ship,—if the
carpenter or the cook were to urge upon the crew their
abstract right to choose their captain, a post of honour
and responsibility to which the carpenter or cook, as
ringleader of the mutiny, himself aspired,—the necessity of instantly checking an ambition so injurious to
the welfare and safety of the ship's company would be
manifest. Similar illustrations might be drawn from
the military, and medical, and legal professions. In
all such cases it is obvious to common sense that men
have no abstract right to alter their position in society,
irrespective of positive and relative duties, of law, order,
personal qualifications, and the public good. And
what is true of these sectional parts of society is not
less true of the whole.

On the highest authority of the supreme Lawgiver,

we learn that the powers that be are ordained of Him
—that to resist them is to resist His ordinance—that
rebellion, discontent, the restless desire of change, are
all more or less blameable; and we may be assured
that neither individuals nor nations may disregard
these sacred precepts with impunity. "My son, fear
thou the LORD and the King; and meddle not with
them that are given to change: for their calamity shall
rise suddenly, and who knoweth the ruin of them
both?"* How many of our deluded countrymen have
lately had cause to repent their neglect of this lesson
of Divine wisdom. And one of the wisest of uninspired
men has observed,—"It is good also not to try experiments in states, except the *necessity be urgent,* or the
*utility evident,* and well to beware that it be the reformation that draweth on the change, and not the
*desire of change* that pretendeth the reformation. And
lastly, that the novelty, though it be not rejected, yet
be held for a *suspect,* and, as the scripture saith, that
we make a stand upon the *ancient way,* and then look
about us, and discover what is the straight and right
way, and so to walk in it."—LORD BACON.

Let us then take our stand upon the ancient way of
our own constitution; and before we forsake it, examine
with care and suspicion (as Lord Bacon advises) the
new paths which the adventurous descendants of our
common ancestors have struck out for themselves in
America, and which some in England invite us to
follow. Let us beware of abandoning our real advantages in the wild pursuit of fancied rights, but rather
look before we leap. The important practical question
is not whether the legislature be *chosen* by many or by
comparatively few, but *what kind of legislature* is the
*result* of that choice.

* Prov. xxiv. 21. 1 Sam. xv. 23. Rom. xiii. Heb. xiii. 5.

The advocates of universal suffrage express their horror of what they call " class legislation ;" and yet they propose to do away with the constitutional representation of *various* classes, and to give us in exchange the representation of one class only. For the effect of universal suffrage *in England* would be to give to the class that have the majority in number, and comparatively a small stake in the country, the whole political power. It would separate power from property; and so far from making property a qualification for voting, as it ought to be, would have the contrary effect, by making numbers every thing, and property of no weight whatever in deciding elections. So unnatural a separation of power from property could not long continue. Either the former order of things would be restored, or those that had the power would seize upon the property, and anarchy, plunder, and ruin would ensue.

A parliament chosen by universal suffrage, as it would represent only *one class*, would consequently *misrepresent* the nation.

It is a sound constitutional maxim, that security of property is essential to civilization and the national welfare; and that consequently not those who have no possessions of their own to lose, and may be reckless in the management of public income and expenditure, but that those who, by industry or other lawful means have acquired property, and accordingly contribute most towards the revenue of their country, have the *best practical qualification and general test* of their fitness to elect the managers of the national wealth and affairs.

We shall see whether or not universal suffrage has prevented bribery and corruption in America, and may judge how far it would be likely to do so in England, when we come to consider the election of the President of the United States. How far are these views illus-

trated by the composition of the house of commons?
Does our mode of election practically exclude the men
of highest talent and character from public affairs, which
M. De Tocqueville assures us is the general result of
universal suffrage in America?

When the sons of our nobility and gentry, when
men who have gained the highest literary honours at
the universities or as authors; eminent barristers, able
and prosperous merchants, distinguished officers of the
army and navy, remarkable for their perspicacity of
intellect and decision of character,—when these offer
themselves as candidates for a seat in parliament, is it
with the view of obtaining the petty salary of some
public functionary? Do they not rather expend considerable sums of money in order that they may
have an opportunity of devoting their time and gra-
tuitous services to their country in that sphere of
honourable ambition?

Doubtless it may, and often does happen, that men
of ability who might have been usefully and honourably
distinguished in parliament, are by their lot in life excluded from that career. But where superior talents
for business and debate are combined with integrity of
character and independent fortune, the very qualities
which, in America, would *debar* the man from a statesman's career, would tend to secure his election as a
member of the British parliament. There Burke,
Pitt, Fox, Sheridan, Canning, Wilberforce, Wyndham,
Romilly, and many other statesmen of former and of
modern times, scarcely their inferiors in genius, wisdom, eloquence, patriotism, and philanthropy, have
charmed and enlightened the listening senate, and the
admiring nation, have defended the people's rights and
the royal prerogative. For many generations our most
illustrious commoners have found their way into parliament, have sustained its character by a course of

legislation, in the main, wise and salutary, and by
many great and able measures. The just and noble
sentiments uttered there on important occasions, and
circulated throughout the empire, have kept alive our
love of freedom, have roused the gallant spirit and
generous patriotism of the nation, while valour received
its highest reward in the tribute of praise spoken by
some eminent orator in the name of his country.

But it may be said the house of commons is not
composed throughout of these choice materials. Undoubtedly "the imperial crown does not consist of a single
diamond, it must be held together by baser matter." The
house of commons consists of men of various characters,
talents, information, and pursuits, from the ablest politicians and most eloquent orators, to the useful plod-
ding man of business, who works in committees, and
the country 'squire, who follows his leader and his party
in the same hark forward style that he follows his
hounds. It is an epitome of the better part of British
society, but it represents the whole.

Designing agitators endeavour to persuade the working classes that they are not represented, because
mechanical and agricultural labourers are not members
of parliament. Even among mechanics there is a
necessary division of labour. The ploughman, or the
smith, or the carpenter, who steadily attends to his own
trade, will succeed better than the Jack of all trades,
who is proverbially master of none. Still greater is
the inconsistency between the duties of the statesman
and those of the ploughman and the mechanic, whose
abilities assuredly would be as much misplaced and
misemployed in the senate, as those of the Duke of
Wellington, Sir Robert Peel, and Lord John Russell,
would be at the plough or at the anvil. But when we
have seen the two Mr. Scotts, rising by native talent
and assiduity from a comparatively humble origin, to

the dignified and useful stations which they occupied as Baron Stowell and the Earl of Eldon; when we see Mr. Copley, the son of an eminent painter, becoming the ornament of his college, one of the most powerful and distinguished advocates at the English bar, filling successively nearly every seat of judicial honour in the land, and now Baron Lyndhurst, and for the third time Lord Chancellor of England;—there is proof that individuals of humble station are not debarred from acquiring even the privileges of a peer, and the highest offices and honours of the state.

It not unfrequently happens that an industrious and respectable farmer, mechanic, or tradesman, who has given his family a good education, has the proud satisfaction and delight to see his children or his grandchildren becoming prosperous merchants, naval or military officers, physicians, clergymen, barristers, nay taking rank with the ablest and the noblest of the land. And that this should occur in the second or third generation is surely far better both for the individuals themselves, and for the community, than that uneducated men should be exalted into public situations of high trust and responsibility, for which they are not qualified, and where they would effectually mar their own happiness and mismanage the weighty and difficult affairs of the nation. The ancient fable of Phæton's rash attempt to drive the chariot of the sun, by which the ambitious driver perished, and the earth was scorched, is an apt emblem of all such incapable aspirants to power.

To persevering merit the way to prosperous and useful distinction is open in England. Extraordinary genius will sometimes pass from the lowest grade of society to the highest honour in a single lifetime. And it is a mistake to suppose that the people are not properly represented, when their representatives are

men of superior station, who have frequently a refined
and generous sympathy for the privations and hardships of their poorer fellow countrymen, which probably
would not be felt, at least in the same degree, by persons
in their own class of life, if elevated to a seat in parliament. An accurate observation of mankind will lead
to this conclusion. Pharaoh's butler, when he had
been taken from prison to a palace, forgot Joseph, who
had been his companion and his benefactor in the
dungeon. The French convention, whom the people
raised to power from their own ranks, became their
most cruel oppressors.

On the other hand, no negro had a seat in parliament; but Wilberforce and other friends of humanity
became the voluntary advocates of those oppressed but
not unrepresented outcasts, and continued to plead
their cause, until the accursed slave trade and slavery
itself were both abolished throughout the British dominions. In democratic America, however, where
universal suffrage has sent to Congress (as De Tocqueville says) representatives who cannot write correctly,
what have they hitherto done to procure liberty for
the oppressed negro labourers? In one half of the
states of the union slavery exists, and throughout the
whole of them the black population are treated as a
degraded and despised race.

And who in England has recently explored the factories, workshops, and dwellings of artisans in the
manufacturing districts, collecting statistical information relative to the sufferings and diseases produced by
excessive and unhealthy toil, that he might advocate
in parliament the cause of the mechanics and the fac-
tory children? Who has carried his humane enquiries
down to the depths of our mines and collieries, to discover what unheeded hardships orphans have had to
endure in various places, from the workmen to whom

they were apprenticed; what evils females and young
children have had to suffer, their own husbands and
parents consenting, and some of their employers neg-
lecting them ?   He who has done this signal service to
the working classes is not one of themselves, but Earl
Shaftesbury's eldest son, Lord Ashley.  While agitators
for selfish ends have deluded the people with their mischievous schemes for repealing the union, and changing
the monarchy into a republic, Lord Ashley has sought
out the real grievances of these afflicted people; and
pitying their distresses, their ignorance, their irreligion,
has made them known to parliament, has struck at the
very root of this enormous evil, which will now be
removed; and he has accomplished these important
and humane reforms, without altering one jot the glorious constitution we inherit from our forefathers.  The
orphan apprentice will no longer be deprived of his
wages; the miner's wife will be restored to her proper
place and duties at home; and the little children will
be allowed to go to school, and to enjoy the sports of
childhood in the light and sunshine of the upper world,
and of their gayest hours, instead of having their young
hearts chilled by cruelty, and their bodies cramped by
labour, and their souls dark as the deep pits in which
they were formerly buried.  And was it to get into
power and place on the shoulders of the multitude, and
to gain a salary for some government situation, that
Lord Ashley became the people's friend ?  No.  When
that disinterested and amiable nobleman was offered a
place in the cabinet, by the present distinguished prime
minister, with whose political principles and Lord
Ashley's there is an entire agreement,  he refused the
honours, rewards, and influence which awaited him, in
order that he might prosecute and urge, without distrac-
tion or restraint, those claims of Christian benevolence,
which he had generously undertaken.

In Lord Ashley, the working classes may recognize a proper specimen of a British member of parliament—the steadfast and disinterested friend of themselves and their children—a noble friend, who neither deludes them by flattery, nor inflames them by agitation—who exacts for his services no *annual tribute;* but, on the contrary, has renounced power, emolument, and fame, that he might continue to do them good.

As the nation is not at all times equally fertile in minds of the highest order, so neither is the house of commons; but viewing it in the aggregate, and for a series of years, it is not surpassed,—may we not say, without partiality or exaggeration ?—it is not equalled by any representative assembly in the world.

And such a house of commons is essential to the right government of this great nation, so elevated in rank and importance among the kingdoms of the earth, and possessing so immense a colonial empire. A house of commons of an inferior description would be inconsistent with the rest of our institutions, and incapable of conducting aright the momentous affairs which engage the attention of the British parliament.

During an important debate, that legislative assembly presents an appearance in every respect becoming its high character. A distinguished leader of one of the two great parties, who are ranged on either side of the speaker's chair, has risen to address the house. The hum of many voices has ceased, and a deep stillness prevails in the crowded hall, and even in the galleries, where every reporter's pen is in motion, and the strangers are listening anxiously, not a syllable is lost, so distinct and emphatic is the graceful speaker's utterance. He skilfully opens his case, his manner denoting the respect due to his audience, and the ease and freedom of conscious power. His narrative flows on in a clear stream, — objections are answered, — argument

follows argument, mingled with playful sallies of wit and
humour, the bold invective, the keen retort, and occasional bursts of eloquence; while cheers and counter-
cheers accompany the orator's progress, ever deepening
and strengthening, to its full and powerful close.   He
resumes his seat, amid those unanimous plaudits with
which superior ability and eloquence are always greeted.
The listener for gratification and delight has been hurried along irresistibly, and wonders what the member
who has started up on the opposite benches has to say
in reply.   If he is worthy to enter the lists with so
formidable an antagonist, the debate proceeds with un-
abated animation.   If not, his apology to the house,
whom he has moved by his *first* sentences, is lost in
the rush of members into the lobby.

    As debates are sometimes adjourned for several days,
and are often continued till past midnight, it is not surprising that there should be decided symptoms of
impatience, when the house is unprofitably detained
from the dispatch of business and from repose.
Sound and valuable information, though delivered in
a homely style, is received with attention; and there
are speakers whose impressive eloquence has power to
charm that assembly, so fastidiously correct in its
judgment of oratory, even when the debate has been
prolonged till day break.   But parliamentary bores,
whose harangues no other means can curtail, are visited
with the strongest expressions of uneasiness and dis-
pleasure.   All circumstances considered, these occasional ebullitions are pardonable and even necessary,
and they soon yield when the speaker sees fit to interpose.   The self-respect of the house is seen in the
deference which is ever paid to him, who seems to
embody the spirit of order, and can calm the storms of
debate with a few oracular words.

    The unceremonious style in which the house of

commons abridges prolixity, when it is thought the question has been fully discussed, and it is time to divide upon it, would surprise a foreigner unacquainted with our national character and institutions. The struggle between the impatient house and certain members eager and fully charged with undelivered speeches, is strange, laughable, and undignified. One or two members there are, whom the loudest storm of disapprobation only causes, like the traveller in the fable, to wrap their impenetrable cloak around them, and jog on more perseveringly. These scenes occur not unfrequently. I take as a specimen a recent instance, at the close of a debate, on May 24, 1842.

Lord Worsley said he had too much respect for the house, to delay them for any length of time, at this hour of the night. Hon. members had not argued fairly against the proposition of the right honourable baronet. He did not object to high duties, but to a prohibition, and to a lean beast and a valuable beast coming in at the same duty. The noble lord resumed his seat amid loud cries of " divide."

Mr. Villiers rose amid yells and noises of various descriptions, which rendered his first sentences inaudible; and the honourable member made a short speech, without further interruption.

Mr. F. Scott and Mr. Ward made a few remarks, without interruption.

Mr. O. Gore rose to speak, amid uproarious cries of " divide." His first few sentences were, therefore, perfectly inaudible, and he continued for a short time to address the house.

Mr. Hume rose, but the cries which had greeted the few preceding members were insignificant, in comparison of the yells, howls, and " bahs," that emanated from all sides of the house; but the honourable member, nothing daunted, said, if he was not allowed to speak, he should move that the chairman report progress, and ask leave to sit again.   This threat allayed, in some measure, the turmoil; and the honourable member said, he saw several members now interrupting the proceedings, who had taken no previous interest in the motion, and he believed their object in coming was to interrupt the business of the house.   (Renewed cries of " bah.")   It was his intention to support the right honourable baronet, and he should not now have addressed the house, but for the charge of calumny which had been brought forward against honourable members on his side of the house.   He could only say, that if the right honourable baronet was as anxious as he had stated himself to be, that animal food should be cheaper, he would adopt the proper course, and make corn cheaper.   (Loud cries of " Oh !" and " sit down.")   The honourable member, however, continued to stand, and in spite of occasional interruptions, finished his speech. The house divided soon afterwards.

Sometimes sarcastic reproof is applied to chastise tediousness, though perhaps with no greater effect, unless to deter other less hardened offenders from the like transgression.

On the whole, is it not better, both as regards the style of oratory and the dispatch of business, that the house should plainly manifest its approbation or dislike of the sentiments addressed to it, than that its members should have that liberty of unlicensed speaking which exists in the house of representatives at Washington, where a single *speech* is often adjourned for several successive days, and afterwards published as a book? The American orators may therefore be said to " speak volumes."   And as some member of Congress talks on from hour to hour, his brother representatives are writing their letters and reading their newspapers, while his solitary voice resounds amid the rustling of leaves, (not of the forest) or perhaps the snore of some sentinel of liberty slumbering at his post.

The personal quarrels which are sometimes caused by unguarded expressions, in the heat of debate, suggest considerations of a graver character. It is to be lamented that eminent statesmen have engaged in duels, having this origin, thus lending the influence of their example to a practice which it had been more virtuous and more truly brave to resist. No force of custom can ever alter the nature of a crime. Neither the power of public opinion, nor the verdicts of juries, given in opposition to the statute book, can absolve from the sentence of the Divine Lawgiver. Much has been ably and unanswerably written, to prove the absurdity of duelling, as a relic of a superstitious and barbarous age,—its utter inefficacy as a means of redress—its criminality as an act of culpable homicide. The question mainly resolves itself into this—Whether shall we fear and obey God or man ? Here most plainly " the friendship of the world is enmity with God." The Christian's duty is therefore evident. He must avoid giving just cause of offence ; where he has done wrong inadvertently, he must be prompt to make full reparation and a fair apology; and he must not be the vindictive avenger of injuries committed against himself. But, the world's reproach,—who can bear it ? Say rather, " a wounded conscience who can bear?" or what mortal man shall dare, with blood-stained hands, to brave the power and the anger of his Maker, who has commanded, in sacred and solemn words, which no sophistry can evade, " Avenge not yourselves, neither give place unto wrath ; vengeance is mine, I will repay, saith the Lord ?"

Truly, to commit a crime in compliance with a foolish and vicious custom, is a strange mixture of physical hardihood and of moral cowardice. But to make the Divine law, conscience, and our duty, the rule of action, and to adhere to that rule, heaven-supported, with the spirit of a martyr,—that is true nobility of soul, that is high moral courage; and although the world of fashion may inflict her most contemptuous frown upon the man who dares to break her chains, he will be cheered and sustained by the Divine approbation, by the testimony of conscience, and the favour of all good men.

It must be admitted, that whenever the house is apprehensive that angry words spoken in debate will lead to a personal altercation, it is prompt to interpose, to prevent the consequences of the absurd and criminal custom, to which so many gentlemen allow themselves to be in bondage. When the quarrel passes off harmlessly, the contrivances by which the wordy warfare is brought to a peaceful termination, consistently with the laws of honour, are sufficiently amusing. They have been well ridiculed by Mr. Dickens, the author of the humourous Pickwick Papers, in the following passage.

Mr. Blotton (of Aldgate) rose to order. Did the honourable Pickwickian allude to him? (Cries of "Order," "Chair," "Yes," "No," "Go on," "Leave off," &c.)

Mr. Pickwick would not be put up to be put down by clamour. He *had* alluded to the honourable gentleman. (Great excitement.)

Mr. Blotton would only say then, that he repelled the honourable gentleman's false and scurrilous accusation, with profound contempt. (Great cheering.) The honourable gentleman was a hum-bug. (Immense confusion, and loud cries of "chair" and "order.")

Mr. A. Snodgrass rose to order. He threw himself upon the chair. (Hear.) He wished to know whether this disgraceful contest between two members of that club should be allowed to continue. (Hear, hear.)

The Chairman was quite sure the honourable Pick-wickian would withdraw the expression he had just made use of.

Mr. Blotton,—with all possible respect for the chair, was quite sure he would not.

The Chairman felt it his imperative duty to demand of the honourable gentleman, whether he had used the expression, which had just escaped him, in a common sense.

Mr. Blotton had no hesitation in saying that he had not—he had used the word in its Pickwickian sense. (Hear, hear.) He was bound to acknowledge that personally he entertained the highest regard and esteem for the honourable gentleman, he had merely considered him a hum-bug in a Pickwickian point of view. (Hear, hear.)

Mr. Pickwick felt much gratified by the fair, candid, and full explanation of his honourable friend. He begged it to be at once understood, that his own observations had been merely intended to bear a Pick-wickian construction. (Cheers.)

In America they manage these things differently, as will be seen from the following report of a scene in the house of representatives, at Washington, on the 9th September, 1841.

BREACH OF PRIVILEGE.—Whilst Mr. Fillmore was in the midst of a sentence, the reporter (who had noticed Mr. Wise cross over to the seat of Mr. Stanley, and had observed those two gentlemen in conversation, apparently of a very excited character) saw Mr. Wise raise his hand violently and aim a blow at the face of Mr. Stanley, who as instantaneously met or returned it. A violent fight followed, and, in less time than it can be described in this report, a scene of mingled uproar and *fight*, such as the reporter in many years' experience has never witnessed on the floor of the house, ensued.  Messrs. Wise and Stanley were lost to the sight of the reporter in the general rush, whilst Mr. Arnold, of Tennessee, and Mr. Butler, of Kentucky, were noticed in a violent personal struggle, striking at and grappling with each other.  Mr. Dixon, H. Lewis, and Mr. Gilmer, and others, were seen in the midst, endeavouring to quell the disturbance, which had now reached a point at which it seemed impossible to arrest its progress.  The members had rushed from all parts of the hall, some rushing over and others standing upon the table, literally piling themselves one on the other, and several canes were seen by the reporter raised up as if in the act of striking.  The Speaker during this time had resumed the chair informally, but no one paid the least regard to his voice, and he called in vain on the officers, none of whom were observed by the reporter, with the exception of the door-keeper, who was endeavouring to close the doors and windows against the crowd from without, who attempted to rush within the hall.

Then, after some explanations by the combatants,

Mr. Ingersoll rose, and offered the following resolution:—' Resolved, That a special committee be appointed to inquire into the circumstances of the rencontre on the floor of this house, between Mr. Wise and Mr. Stanley, members of this house, and to report thereon to the house.'

Mr. Andrews, of Kentucky, said, that at the *last Congress* a committee had been appointed *on a similar subject* when *a similar occurrence* had taken place. How that investigation ended everybody knew.  He was opposed to the appointment of a committee.  He considered the former occurrence disgraceful to the house, as he considered this.  He thought that the two members engaged deserved to be expelled, and he believed they should be expelled now upon the spot, and without further delay. (Cries in many parts of the house, 'Agreed,' 'Agreed.') There was no other way in which the house could vindicate its character and its dignity. The committee appointed in a similar case at the last Congress had done nothing, had recommended nothing; *and the indignity which had been offered to the house and the country went unpunished and unrebuked.* He was for no committee, it would be a mere whitewashing affair, a mere hum-bug, such as we had heretofore had.

The resolution of Mr. Ingersoll, by ayes one hundred and twenty-four, noes not counted, was adopted.

The affair was afterwards settled by the mutual explanation of the members: and on a subsequent occasion, a boxing match took place in the house, between a Mr. Bell and a Mr. Towney, who apologized in like manner.

The Hon. Augustus Murray relates that a colonel and a general, who were relations, and both members of the American legislature, having quarrelled, the colonel struck the general, who challenged him, leaving the colonel the choice of weapons. The colonel knowing the general to be an expert swordsman and an unerring shot, proposed that he and the general should both sit on the same barrel of gunpowder, and by applying a match settle all their differences with one grand blow up. The general declined the invitation, and they finally agreed to fight with muskets at five or ten paces. The colonel was wounded in the wrist, and the general was shot through the heart.

Mr. Murray says, the incident derives some importance, as the parties were in respectable and responsible stations, and the circumstances were related to him in a manner rather laudatory of the courage than condemnatory of the thirst of blood displayed. He also quotes from the New Orleans newspapers the following statement :—" On the 3rd of February, 1835, a little before the usual time of meeting of the house of representatives, Mr. J. Grymes, a distinguished lawyer of New Orleans, entered the hall, and advancing towards Mr. Labranche, the speaker of the house, raised his cane and struck him, whereupon Mr. Labranche drew a pistol and fired at Mr. Grymes. The ball passed through the lappet of his coat; he immediately drew a pistol and fired at Mr. Labranche who fell wounded. After a long dispute as to the right of the house to try Mr. Grymes for this assault, it was carried in the affirmative, and he was brought up to the bar and *reprimanded.*"

Mr. Dickens's work contains many similar incidents that occurred, principally in the slave-holding states.

Thus it appears that universal suffrage and the ballot introduce into the American houses of representatives some legislators who, when arguments fail, have recourse to blows. We have had no boxing matches or assassinations hitherto in the house of commons, and it is to be hoped never will; but let us beware how we open the doors of parliament, by annual elections, ballot, and universal suffrage, to the advocates and admirers of " physical force."

The senates and houses of representatives in the state legislatures being all elected by the people, and only for short periods, are nearly on a par with each other. But the senate of the supreme government is elected in a different manner. The *legislature* of each state of the union returns two members to the senate at Washington, the entire number at present being fifty-two.

What is the character of that assembly ?   " There are in the senate a great proportion of men of experience, of sound ability, and who would do credit to any nation upon earth."—FEARON, p. 313.   M. De

Tocqueville's description, twenty years afterwards, is as follows, and it accords with the statements of still more recent travellers. "A few paces from the house of representatives is the hall of the senate which, in a small space, contains a great part of what is most celebrated in America. You scarcely see a member who is unknown to fame. There are eloquent barristers, distinguished generals, able magistrates, eminent statesmen. The speeches in this assembly would do honour to the first parliamentary debates in Europe."

What then is the fair inference to be drawn from the decided superiority of the senate of the federal government to all other legislative bodies in the United States? That even in America, where property is far more generally distributed than in the states of the old world, and the conditions and qualifications for government are also more nearly on a level, universal suffrage is a rude and clumsy electoral machine, producing an inferior result. But when elected bodies become the electors of another assembly, by this second process a finer and a better product is obtained, rendering the failure of the former mode of election so much the more evident. Still less would universal suffrage harmonize with our institutions; and to those who imagine it would, the following remark of M. De Tocqueville, a writer avowedly partial to democratic governments, although acute in discovering their defects, and singularly candid in exposing them, may serve as a useful warning. "It is easy," he says, " to descry in the future, a period when the American republics will be forced to multiply election by two degrees in their electoral system, under the penalty of being miserably entangled amid the rocks and shoals of democracy."

The senate of congress is, doubtless, the most

illustrious assembly in the United States, and their
wisdom and firmness have hitherto done much to preserve their country from being wrecked on those rocks
and shoals of democracy, which M. De Tocqueville
perceives in the distance. President Adams, Washington's immediate successor, relied on the senate for
restraining the people. "No republic," said Mr. Adams,
" can ever be of any duration without a senate, and a
senate deeply and strongly rooted—strong enough to
bear up against all popular storms and passions.
Hitherto the senate have done well, but probably they
will be *forced to give way in time.*"—JEFFERSON's
*Memoirs,* Vol. III. p. 383.

If the senators had been elected for life, and with a
considerable property qualification, as General Hamilton is understood to have proposed, the stability and
independence of the senate would have been greater;
but, according to its present constitution, it too nearly
resembles the house of representatives, and is almost as
much influenced by the popular will. M. De Tocqueville
says that in America, the wealthier classes are not
united by any common tie : and that the bench and
the bar form the only aristocracy. Lawyers are generally well educated, trained to severe study, to reasoning
and debate. Then the law of England, which forms
the basis of American jurisprudence, is founded on
precedents, and the lawyers must be guided by statutes
and decisions. It will be afterwards explained how
every question of constitutional law comes under the
review of the American judges, who consequently have
a degree of political influence, which is denied to the
English judges. For these and other reasons, M. De
Tocqueville considers the American bench and bar to
be the only aristocracy of the country. And, he says,
" without this admixture of lawyer-like sobriety with
the democratic principle, I question whether democratic

institutions could long be maintained; and I cannot believe that a republic could subsist at the present time, if the influence of lawyers, in public business, did not increase in proportion to the power of the people :"—a slender hope for republican institutions.

The position which the senate occupies in the American constitution corresponds to that of the upper house of the British parliament, and in some respects they are analogous. The house of lords contains the Marlboroughs and the Wellingtons of history, victorious in the field and wise in council; great and successful naval heroes; judges, formerly eminent at the bar, who have attained the highest dignities of their profession—acute to discover in the bills which originate in either house, whatever is objectionable in principle or in detail, able to comprehend how far they are consistent with constitutional law, and the whole range of our jurisprudence.

Prejudiced and uninformed persons may be unable or unwilling to perceive the great value of a revision of the measures of the house of commons by the house of lords. But innumerable are the instances in which the alteration of bills by the peers, the sending of them back for reconsideration with strong reasons for amendment, and the total rejection of them when radically bad, have guarded the constitution from innovation, and the statute book from absurdity. Distinguished statesmen, already trained to business and debate in the house of commons and in various public offices, are elevated to the house of lords, after the first fervours of their early political opinions have abated, and their views have been matured by years and experience. And it is of great advantage to themselves and to the country, that the sons of peers undergo that valuable training in the lower house; and are often eminently distinguished there, before succeeding to the rank which entitles them to a seat in the house of lords.

Since human nature and human institutions are imperfect, it cannot be affirmed that there are among the peers none unworthy of their dignity, uninjured by the temptations of rank, wealth, and luxury,— no "tenth transmitters of a foolish face." It is from occasional instances of unworthiness and dishonour, that the scoffers at hereditary honours derive their most successful arguments; and the very zeal with which such cases are censured and stigmatized shews how strongly the influence of public opinion is brought to bear on the whole aristocratic body.

But if high birth does open a path in which there is many a snare and pitfall for heedless youth and profligate manhood, it is, nevertheless, the way to honour and renown. While most men must wait for opportunities of distinction that may never arrive, the nobleman is born, in some measure, a public character, and the natural course of his life flows on to fortune. If endowed with good talents and dispositions, and educated as becomes his station, he is destined from his boyhood to occupy situations of great influence and usefulness. Others must slowly climb and toil up the steep ascent, which he gained in youth's freshness or in manhood's prime.

Is it no benefit to be the lineal descendant of ancestors whose names and actions are celebrated in history, to be nurtured among those to whom ease and dignity are almost second nature, and the elegance that fashion copies is an inborn grace; to stand upon an eminence seen and observed by all men, where vice and folly are exposed to greater shame, and from which wisdom and virtue shed their lustre afar? Will not such elevation, motives, education, ennoble and advantage many,— though some few are degenerate? Whether do we expect the courser, known by his pedigree, or the sluggish ignoble dray to be foremost in the race?

A body like the British peerage, limited in number, and distinguished by peculiar honours, has a character and special privileges to maintain. Were it elected by the people most of its advantages would be lost. If it could not be increased by new creations, it would become an object of jealousy to the country and would degenerate. But the sovereign having the prerogative of introducing commoners into the ranks of the nobility as a reward for public services, their order attracts to itself, from age to age, whatever is most illustrious in the state. Beyond the difficulties and dangers which they encountered in their country's service, and through the clouds of battle, how many a lofty spirit, like Nelson, has seen a peerage and Westminster abbey in the vista of fame!

The peers being associated together, with such high privileges and responsibilities, form an admirable counterpoise to the fickleness of the irresponsible multitude; tempering the zeal and regulating the eccentricities of popular opinion. They oppose a compact barrier to encroachments of the sovereign, and to the usurpation of powerful individuals. When the barons obtained magna charta, they secured privileges not for their own order only but also for the people.

When some great general gains victory after victory, at the head of the national armies, he receives the successive steps of aristocratic dignity, and ample is his reward. Greater he could not be were he to usurp the throne; nay, at that attempt his glory would vanish, and the rest of the nobility would instantly rally round their hereditary monarch, to defeat and punish the traitor. Never did one thought of treason to his sovereign and his country enter the mind of that truly great man, who has passed through every degree of military and civil dignity, with unequalled glory, and with the native integrity, sincerity, and simplicity of his noble mind untarnished. Far more honourable than Napoleon's usurped imperial diadem, are the laurel wreath and the ducal coronet that grace the brow of England's veteran patriot—her beloved and revered WELLINGTON. In this respect, so admirable are our institutions, that while every motive is held out to the great and good to serve their country, there is really no temptation to play the part of a traitor and a military usurper.

In the commonwealth there is a natural gradation of interests, from the sovereign to the humblest man that subsists by his daily toil. But if it be asked what class, in proportion to its numbers, has the strongest interest in the national welfare? we reply, the aristocracy. The labourer may emigrate, the merchant too may convey his wealth and carry on his trade abroad, and the landed proprietor may sell his estate, and quit his native land; but the nobleman, both by his title and his family possessions, is strongly attached to his country. Therefore the nobility are peculiarly the natural guardians of the state. From their elevated position, and by their strong interest in its weal or woe, they are quick to discern approaching evils; and whether they come from foreign enemies, from arbitrary acts of the crown, from the ambition of powerful subjects, or the violence of the people, the peers are ready to sound the alarm, and to ward off the danger. What then shall be said of the miserable sophism, that because the house of lords is not elected by the people, therefore it has no sympathy with the nation at large. Have not the peers and the people both an interest in the welfare of the country? and is not the interest of the house of lords, in proportion to its numbers, far greater than that of any other class? But further, the sons of peers are commoners. By the intermarriages of the nobility and gentry, the two classes are intermingled. And so throughout English society, there

are various degrees linked together; while in America
there is an almost homogeneous mass, acted upon by
sudden commotion, without interruption, barrier, or
controul. In England, what agitates the people, affects
indeed the hereditary, and also the natural aristocracy
of the country; namely, the aristocracy of wealth, talent,
and learning: but all are not agitated in the same
manner and to the same extent. In America, the
nation is all people. In England it consists of various
orders united, sympathizing, yet not identical. The
higher and more privileged in their own persons, and
the subordinate, either by themselves or their representatives, share in the local or general government.
Those that rule are accustomed also to obey. The
highest is not above the laws, whose just and humane
arrangements afford protection and provision for the
poorest. There is neither the arbitrary master nor the
abject slave. The admirable tendency of our institutions and customs is to preserve all in their proper
places, to allow great activity and freedom, but to prevent injustice and violence. The constitution of society
in this country we deem to be in unison with the material structure and moral government of the universe,
in which " one star differeth from another star in glory;"
and from the highest to the lowest of created things,
there are diversities of being and of power; the mutually dependent parts of one grand harmonious system.

The house of lords is not indeed formed at the hustings; yet it has a national origin, although by a slower
and more refined process than *popular election ;*—by a
process which may be illustrated by the production of
the topmost boughs of a tree, that yield the fairest
blossoms and the choicest fruit. Because their growth
was gradual, not the less perfect is their union with the
parent stem. And so the peers have union and sympathy with the nation, whence they sprung, by the

gradual growth and efflorescence of its greatness and its glory.

We believe that the house of lords is unrivalled by any other legislative assembly in the world, in dignity, in talent, in calm deliberative wisdom. From the house of commons it must be expected that the nation will principally receive those impulses by which it moves onward through successive stages of advancing civilization. But the house of lords gives to that progress a safe direction, checks its velocity, tempers its rashness, moderates the innovating spirit of the times, and moulds the fresh workmanship of the legislator of the day into better agreement with the ancient and venerable fabric of our laws and constitution. That which President Adams desired for his country, Englishmen already enjoy—they have a senate " deeply and strongly rooted, strong enough to bear up against all popular storms and passions." If the house of lords were to yield to clamour, and to refrain from the exercise of its proper functions,—as some men, wise in their own conceit, have suggested,—an essential organ of the constitution would become weak and ineffectual, and the balance of its admirable mechanism would be destroyed. If the people were to elect a house of commons, ignorant or regardless of the past course of legislation, who should endeavour to subvert our laws and institutions by frequent and unconstitutional changes, the house of lords would arrest the ruinous course of affairs, until haply the nation should return to better and wiser counsels.

Marlborough, Chatham, Cornwallis, Mansfield, Nelson, Wellington,—the very names of the nobility, what eventful times, what scenes of greatness and of glory do they summon up to our remembrance! The people possibly might forget, or be so infatuated as to despise, the most memorable occurrences, the most instructive lessons of British history; but never can the peers forget, whose titles, heraldic ensigns, and family records, are so many proud memorials of renown. When called to deliberate, at some dangerous and signal crisis, as constitutional guardians not only of their own privileges, but also of the throne, the church, the common welfare, the national glory, have the peers ever deserted their country in the hour of peril ? Although anarchy, with stormy billows, should rise and swell around the vessel of the state, would not they, animated by the spirit of their sires, either perish with her in the waves, or bring her back to her accustomed course and haven in safety, having taken their fixed, their hereditary resolve, " We will never change the constitution and the laws of England!"

# THE EXECUTIVE POWER.

## LECTURE IV.

The President of the United States—The British Sovereign
—Their ministers—Elections—Elective and hereditary
monarchy—The veto—Mutual relations of the executive
and the legislature in both countries—How far these have
been affected in England by the Reform bill—Opinions of
American statesmen respecting the British constitution.

EACH state of the union having a separate legislature,
the sovereignty is divided between the states and the
federal government. The President of the United
States is only the executive organ of the *federal government*, to which the state legislatures, as we have
seen, are not uniformly submissive. But the British
Sovereign wields the executive power of the whole
nation; and the vigour which is necessary to rule an
empire, situated in every quarter of the globe, is unim-
paired by the insubordination of conflicting authorities.

The President may convoke Congress on extraordinary occasions, but cannot dissolve it. Ordinarily it
meets, adjourns, and is dissolved, without his interpo-
sition.

The British Sovereign summons, prorogues, and
dissolves parliament; a privilege designed to protect
the monarchy, and to prevent the legislature from

perpetuating and abusing its great power, as the Long Parliament did in the reign of Charles the First.

The President is personally responsible for the measures of his ministers. But in England, the person of the Sovereign is deemed sacred and inviolable, while his ministers are made responsible for their acts, done in his name.

The President cannot conclude treaties without the sanction of two-thirds of the senate. Like the British Monarch, he is commander-in-chief of the army and navy; but the American army consists only of about six thousand regular soldiers, and its navy is much less numerous than ours.

The President's veto is only suspensive. If he objects to any measure of Congress, he may send it back, with his objections, to the house where it originated, to be reconsidered. If two-thirds of that house agree to pass the bill, it is sent to the other house, and if there also it is approved by two-thirds, the bill becomes law.

It is consistent with the high dignity of the British Sovereign, that his veto should be absolute. But it is a power vested in him for extraordinary occasions, and in the admirable working of our constitution, the struggle is made in parliament, and is decided without having recourse to the royal veto.

The American President is elected for four years only. He is not *directly* chosen by the people, nor yet by Congress; but by delegates specially appointed, as follows.—The whole body of electors choose as many delegates as they return representatives to Congress: these delegates do not assemble together, but vote in their respective states. Three candidates may be proposed, and he who has the majority of votes is appointed the President. If no one candidate has a majority, the house of representatives at Washington determine which of the three shall be elected. This arrangement has been admirably contrived, to produce the least possible excitement and delay in the choice of the supreme magistrate—for the President is only a chief magistrate, and the executive power is almost wholly absorbed by the representatives of the people in Congress. This evil was apprehended by the ablest and wisest of the statesmen who framed the constitution. General Hamilton, in the Federalist, a masterly work, to which he was the chief contributor, in treating of the tendency of the popular branch of the legislature to absorb every other, says, "In governments purely republican, this tendency is almost irresistible." The history of his country, since the decease of that wise and patriotic statesman, has evinced his foresight.

The official authority of the American President is only the shadow of regal power. He must have respect to local and sectional interests, in the appointment of the ministers of state, and consequently is not free to choose the best. The ministers are jealously excluded from Congress.

But in England it is considered necessary that the cabinet ministers should sit in parliament, and be conversant with all its proceedings. They must be ready to explain and defend their measures, before a vigilant and active opposition, zealous to expose every error, fraud, and inconsistency of the party in power. Nothing but sterling talent and integrity—a wise, constitutional, and vigorous course of policy, can stand the test of this public scrutiny, which affords a most powerful motive to the faithful and laborious discharge of ministerial duties, and the best possible safeguard against corruption, negligence, and incapacity.

But the American ministers of state are required to burrow in their government offices. For high crimes and misdemeanours they may be impeached, while minor official delinquencies may escape detection and punishment.    Mr. Fearon relates that his brother radical, the well known Wm. Cobbett, declared that during the several *years* which he resided near the Treasury, in London, he " did not witness so much bribery, corruption, and place hunting, as he had seen in one week in Pennsylvania."    Mr. Fearon says, although he cannot go the length of Mr. Cobbett and his friend, in their wholesale censures, perhaps from not having had the same opportunity with them of forming a judgment, " Yet I have become acquainted with facts in Washington, which no man could have induced me to believe without personal observation."    And Mr. Buckingham, a very recent traveller, who has visited many other foreign countries, says, " In no country which I have visited, has such an array of delinquencies committed by men in confidential public situations been exhibited, as has met my eye since I came to the United States."

The communications of the American ministers with Congress are not made orally, but in writing.    Consequently, unprofitable debates often arise, for want of such immediate explanations as our ministers are called upon to give, in their places in parliament.    And further, by a practical alteration of the American constitution, Congress has assumed in a great measure the power of the officers of state.    The committees of the British house of commons do not exercise any functions not properly belonging to the house itself.    They are appointed to investigate various public questions and private bills, and they report to the house the result of their investigations.    But the American Congress appoints committees for finance, for foreign affairs, and other departments of the executive government, from which the ministers who have charge of them are excluded.    Those committees manage, in a great measure, the business of the country; and bills brought into Congress without their approbation, would probably not pass. In the United States then, the President and his ministers are excluded from the legislature and its committees, which absorb the essential power of the executive.

But in Great Britain the ministers form the government,—are constitutionally checked by the parliament, and are responsible to the nation. To the scrutiny and decision of parliament—to the observation of the country, and the discussion of a free press—all their measures are openly submitted; and thus the executive and the legislature work together with fewer abuses, with more effect, and with greater harmony.

The President of the United States may be re-elected. To prohibit this would be to deprive the nation in many cases of the services of a man of talent, after they had become more valuable by his experience. But the defects of the American executive are still more obvious on the second election of the President, to secure which he is allured to mingle in the intrigues of his partizans—to stoop to popular arts—to fetter himself with pledges and promises—to misemploy his power and patronage, and to govern with a view to gain the suffrages by which his term of authority may be prolonged. The constitution has placed him in the situation of a tenant at will, who is anxious to renew his lease of office; it tempts him to act in the spirit of the unjust steward in the sacred parable—" I am resolved what to do, that when I am put out of the stewardship they may receive me into their houses."

As regards the President, his ministers and the American statesmen generally, the *tendency* of this system is unfavourable to comprehensive and far-sighted plans of government,—to an independent, generous, and noble course of conduct,—to legislation for the best and highest interests of the community and of posterity. Such is its tendency, though upright and distinguished men may resist it.

Long previous to the election of a President, the nation is occupied in preparing for the event, and the course of government is for awhile arrested. Mr. Jefferson wrote to a friend, about six weeks before the expiration of his term of office, that, beyond the expression of his opinion, he took no part in public affairs, deeming it right to allow his successor to begin those measures of which he must superintend the execution. And the ministers, and other officers appointed by the President, go out along with him. The President's is the most important and the most agitating of all the elections. The United States are convulsed every four years by that political earthquake, which in countries less favourably situated would be very disastrous in its effects, and is less injurious in America only in consequence of its immense extent, and its remoteness from Europe. The American chancellor Kent has observed that if ever the peace of the union is to be "jeopardised by the struggle for power, it will be upon this very subject of the election of the President."

But the annual and biennial elections of the representatives in Congress, and the members of the several state legislatures, keep up the excitement of party strife, whose concentrated violence bursts forth at that great political crisis. Here, therefore, I shall state all I have to say on the subject of the American elections generally.

The President's election of 1828 was thus alluded to by Governor Clinton, in his annual message to the legislature, quoted in Captain Hall's Travels. " Party spirit has entered the recesses of retirement, violated the sanctity of female character, invaded the tranquillity of private life, and visited with severe inflictions the peace of families. Neither elevation nor humility has been spared, nor the charities of life, nor distinguished public services, nor the fire-side, nor the altar, have been left free from attack, but a licentious and destroying spirit has gone forth." The New York Annual Register says further: "that even the tomb was not held sacred from the rancorous hostility which distinguished the Presidential election of 1828." In New York the Irish emigrants are about 40,000 in number. One of these Irishmen told Captain Marryatt that he had voted seven times in the different wards during the same election. His countrymen are sufficiently numerous to carry the election at New York, which has greater influence than any other state in determining the election of the President. The tide of emigration flows on steadily, and the descendants and connections of the Irish emigrants, and other members of the church of Rome, are rapidly acquiring immense political influence in America. The New York election, in 1838, (ten years afterwards) is thus mentioned by one of the *whig* papers. "Some of the wards threw from *four to six hundred more votes than there were known to be resident in them.* Double voting was practised to the greatest extent. The whole spirit of the naturalization laws was defied, and an utter mockery was made of the sacred right of suffrage. What party is likely to be most guilty of these things may be judged from the fact that the loco-foco party resist every proposition for a registry law, *or any other law,* that will give the people a fair, and honest, and constitutional system of voting." So writes the whig-democratic editor of his brethren the loco-focos, or ultra democrats. But notwithstanding these nefarious proceedings the whig-democrats gained the election. Was it by abstaining from the base and corrupt arts of their opponents? Was it by the triumph of that higher principle and immaculate purity, which some suppose is to be found in perfection only in that trans-Atlantic land of liberty, where democracy reigns with its triple crown of annual elections, universal suffrage, and the ballot, over a free, and a *sovereign* people? By no means. An influential whig, in his exultation at the success of his own party on this occasion, told Captain Marryatt, "We beat them, sir, *literally* with their own *weapons*. We bought over all their bludgeon men, at so many dollars per head, and the very sticks intended to be used to keep *us* from the poll were employed upon the heads of the loco-focos." Here we find the art of governing mankind reduced to its primitive and rude simplicity, by the old summary method of an outward appeal to the understanding of a wrong-headed opponent. But surely such realities must disappoint the fond hopes of those who have pictured America as a land of pure liberty, where dollars never could be employed to corrupt the integrity of the patriotic voter, nor bludgeons be used to break—his independence. Thus it is that

" Distance lends enchantment to the view,"

and the illusions of fancy are dispelled by the lessons of experience.

In England, elections are happily confined to the choice of members of parliament, and all the legislative enactments, which have been employed to prevent bribery and treating, have not hitherto been sufficient to eradicate the unconstitutional abuses of this popular right, and their demoralizing influence. The disclosures which have taken place during the last session of parliament, regarding the bribery and corruption which occurred at the general election in 1841, ought to make us blush for our national character. In this respect, truly, we have no right to find fault with the Americans. How can we see clearly the mote in our brother's eye, when there is such a beam in our own eye? But it is gratifying to observe that both the government and the leading members of the house of commons have more earnestly striven to grapple with these flagrant abuses, and, if possible, to destroy them. May they be successful—that purity of election may be restored according to the theory of our glorious constitution, which many have set aside in practice; for the root of the evil is not in the constitution, neither will it be cured by any violation of the constitution. Bribery and corruption, and bludgeon men, are employed in America, where there are short parliaments, the ballot, and universal suffrage. And what has the extension of the franchise done for us in this country? It may have diminished the amount of each particular bribe, but the number of bribes it has increased. Corruption and immorality, instead of being concentrated, have been diffused. Thus, whether the electors be many or few, whether they be in England or in America, whether they live under a monarchy or a democracy, bribery and corruption are found to prevail. What does this prove, but that the evil has its source and centre not merely in the political constitution of either country, but in the moral constitution of man? And as one of the greatest and best of the German reformers said, he found the old Adam was too strong for young Melancthon, so here the old Adam will be too strong for the most zealous political reformers. They may discourage and check the evil by such preventive means as they are now adopting, but purity of election can never be attained until the motives and actions of candidates, and canvassers, and electors, shall become more pure. Men must renounce the jesuitical maxim, that the end justifies the means—they must do away with the false distinction between their moral conscience and their political conscience—they must scorn to do, collectively

in committees, and secretly by the agency of others,
what, as honest upright men, they would refuse to do
in their own persons, and what they would blush to
confess before their country.

The duration of the exciting scenes of elections has
been very beneficially limited to one or two days; and,
although they give opportunity for the display of much
vice and folly, they do not endanger the peace of the
country. Having treated the subject gravely, a short
extract, in a lighter strain, from the Pickwick Papers,
will recal to mind the principal arts and abuses of
electioneering, which, most deservedly, come under
the lash of the satirist. " The stable-yard exhibited
unequivocal symptoms of the glory and strength of the
Eatanswill blues. There was a regular army of blue
flags, some with one handle, and some with two,
exhibiting appropriate devices, in golden characters,
four feet high, and stout in proportion. There was a
grand band of trumpets, bassoons, and drums, mar-
shalled four abreast, and earning their money, if ever
men did, especially the drum-beaters, who were very
muscular. There were bodies of constables, with blue
staves, twenty committee men with blue scarfs, and a
mob of voters, with blue cockades. There were electors
on horseback, and electors a-foot. There was an open
carriage-and-four for the Honourable Samuel Slumkey,
and there were four carriages and pair for his friends
and supporters; and the flags were rustling, and the
band was playing, and the twenty committee men were
squabbling, and the mob were shouting, and the
horses were backing, and the post-boys perspiring,
and every body, and every thing then and there
assembled, was for the special use, behoof, honour, and renown, of the Honourable Samuel
Slumkey of Slumkey, Hall, one of the candidates
for the representation of the borough of Eatanswill,

in the commons' house of parliament of the United Kingdom.

"Is every thing ready?" said the Hon. Samuel Slumkey to Mr. Perker.

"Every thing, my dear sir," was the little man's reply.

"Nothing has been omitted, I hope?" said the Hon. Samuel Slumkey.

"Nothing has been left undone, my dear sir, nothing whatever. There are twenty *washed* men at the street-door for you to shake hands with, and six children in arms that you are to pat on the head, and inquire the age of; be particular about the children, my dear sir— it has always a great effect, that sort of thing."

"I'll take care," said the Hon. Samuel Slumkey.

"And, perhaps, my dear sir," said the cautious little man, "perhaps, if you *could*—I don't mean to say it's indispensable,—but if you *could* manage to *kiss* one of 'em, it would produce a very great impression on the crowd."

"Would'nt it have as good an effect if the proposer or seconder did that?" said the Hon. Samuel Slumkey.

"Why I am afraid it wouldn't," replied the agent; "if it were done by yourself, my dear sir, I think it would make you very popular."

"Very well," said the Hon. Samuel Slumkey, with a resigned air, "then it must be done—that's all."

During the whole time of the polling the town was in a perpetual fever of excitement. Every thing was conducted on the most liberal and delightful scale. Exciseable articles were remarkably cheap at all the public-houses; and spring vans paraded the streets, for the accommodation of voters who were seized with any temporary dizziness in the head—an epidemic which prevailed among the electors, during the contest, to a most alarming extent, and under the influence of which they might be seen lying on the pavement in a state of utter insensibility. A small body of electors remained unpolled on the very last day. They were calculating and reflecting persons, who had not yet been convinced by the arguments of either party, although they had had frequent conferences with each. One hour before the close of the poll, Mr. Perker solicited the honour of a private interview with these intelligent, these noble, these patriotic men. It was granted. His arguments were brief, but satisfactory. They went in a body to the poll; and when they returned, the Honourable Samuel Slumkey, of Slumkey Hall, was returned also."

If those demagogues, who have proposed to render the house of commons more democratic, and to deprive the house of lords of their hereditary privileges, were to complete their revolutionary scheme by proposing to make the British monarchy elective, we need only glance at the relative circumstances of England and America in order to be satisfied, that convulsions which are so perilous even in the United States, at the election of a President, would, in this country, produce the speedy and inevitable ruin of our institutions and our empire. The object contended for in America is an office of very limited power, and very short duration. But only set up as the prize for ambition the crown and sceptre of a mighty kingdom, and civil wars and bloody revolutions would desolate the country, and foreigners, as in ancient and more barbarous times, would be allured to interfere in aid of one or other of the combatants. The advocates of such a scheme would scarcely recommend it by referring to the elections of the Cæsars, during the decline of the Roman empire, when the imperial purple was awarded by the voice of a military mob, and often conferred by means of assassination and civil war. Neither would the precedent avail them of the election of the popes, where the candidate and electors are ecclesiastics, and the priestly hierarchy and the monarchy are identical; and where, on the death of a pope, recourse is not indeed had to arms—but nepotism, the sale of offices, and manifold intrigues are employed to determine what aged cardinal shall be raised to the papal throne, which is modestly called a chair.

The question of an elective monarchy for England does not deserve an argument: but let us just imagine three rival candidates taking the field in a contest for the British crown, and striving who should first gain over the army or obtain possession of the navy,—or secure the metropolis or rouse the peasantry,—while one of them heads a rebellion in Ireland, to make himself king. When the country is rent asunder with furious factions and civil war, our foreign foes are seen assembling their forces in the distance. This imaginary picture is improbable, only because it is unlikely that we shall ever be so infatuated as to make the fatal experiment of electing our Kings.

The declaration of right was prepared by that distinguished whig nobleman, Lord Somers, and it distinctly sets forth the great principle of the hereditary succession to the throne—"that on the preserving a *certainty* in the succession thereof, the unity, peace, and tranquillity of this nation doth, under God, wholly depend."

"So far," says Burke, "is it from being true, that we acquired a right, by the revolution, to elect our kings, that if we had possessed it before, the English nation did at that time most solemnly renounce and abdicate it for themselves and all their posterity for ever.

"At no time, perhaps, did the sovereign legislature manifest a more tender regard to that fundamental

principle of British constitutional policy than at the
time of the revolution, when it deviated from the direct
line of hereditary succession.    The crown was carried
somewhat out of the line in which it had before moved,
but the new line was derived from the same stock.    It
was still a line of hereditary descent; still an hereditary
descent in the same blood, though an hereditary
descent qualified with *protestantism*.  When the legislature altered the direction, but kept the *principle*, they
shewed that they held it inviolable."—*Reflections on
the French Revolution.*

In the event of the death of the President, during
his term of office, the Vice President immediately
succeeds to him, an arrangement necessary to prevent
the state from being left for some time without a
chief magistrate.    This event has very lately occurred,
for the first time in the history of the United States,
by the succession of Vice President Tyler to General
Harrison. It is singular that the Vice President, holding
opposite views to his predecessor on the great party
question of the day—the incorporation of the United
States Bank,—has pronounced his veto *in opposition* to
the voice of the majority who elected General Harrison.
This is a strange anomaly in the American institutions,
which has just manifested itself.  In England the royal
prerogatives are exercised with the advice and concur-
rence of a responsible ministry, and practically the
veto is in abeyance.  On the contrary, President Tyler
has exercised his veto, with regard to the proceedings
of Congress, four or five times in about a twelvemonth,
and the American legislature and executive are at
present at variance with each other.

The committee of the house of representatives has
given in a report to Congress, which the President, in
a protest just issued by him, says, " has assailed my
whole official conduct, without a shadow of a pretext

for such assault; and stopping short of impeachment, has charged me nevertheless with offences declared to deserve impeachment. ·Had the extraordinary report," he continues, " which the committee thus made to the house, been permitted to remain without the sanction of the latter, I should not have uttered a regret or complaint upon the subject. But, unaccompanied as it is by any particle of testimony to support the charges it contains, without a deliberate examination, almost without any discussion, the house of representatives has been pleased to adopt it as its own, and, thereby, to become my accuser before the country and before the world. ............ I am not only subjected to imputations affecting my character as an individual, but am charged with offences against the country so grave and so heinous, as to deserve public disgrace and disfranchisement. I am charged with *violating pledges which I never gave,* and, because I execute what *I believe to be the law,* with usurping powers not conferred by law; and, above all, with using the powers conferred upon the President by the constitution, from corrupt motives and for unwarrantable ends; and these charges are made without *any particle of evidence* to sustain them, and, as I solemnly affirm, *without any foundation in truth.*

" I protest against this whole proceeding of the house of representatives, as *ex parte* and extra judicial. I protest against it, as subversive of the common right of all citizens to be condemned only upon a fair and impartial trial, according to law and evidence, before the country. I· protest against it, as destructive of all comity of intercourse between the departments of this government, and destined, sooner or later, to lead to *conflicts fatal to the peace of the country, and the integrity of the constitution.* I protest against it, in the name of that constitution, which is not only my own

shield of protection and defence, but that of every American citizen. I protest against it, in the name of the people, by whose will I stand where I do, and by whose authority I exercised the power which I am charged with having usurped, and to whom I am responsible for a firm and faithful discharge, according to my own convictions of duty, of the high stewardship confided to me by them. I protest against it, in the name of all regulated liberty, and all limited government, as a proceeding tending to the *utter destruction of the checks and balances of the constitution, and the accumulating in the hands of the house of representatives, or a bare majority of Congress,* for the time being, of an *uncontrouled and despotic power.* And I respectfully ask that this, my protest, may be entered upon the journal of the house of representatives, as a solemn and formal declaration, for all time to come, of the injustice and unconstitutionality of such a proceeding.  " JOHN TYLER.
" WASHINGTON, *August* 30, 1842."

Such unseemly and dangerous collision between the legislature and the executive government tells its own tale.

The President's position is not sufficiently independent to run the risk of unpopularity, by offering honest but unpalatable advice. The prevailing tone of the addresses of the Presidents is therefore homage to the people. A few extracts from the inaugural address of General Harrison, in March, 1841, will illustrate these remarks, and throw light on some points of the American constitution.—" The broad foundation upon which our constitution rests being the people—a *breath* of theirs having made, as a breath can unmake, change, or modify it—it can be assigned to none of the great divisions of government, but to that of *democracy.* .........
We admit of no government by Divine right, believing,

that, so far as power is concerned, the beneficent **Creator** has made *no distinction amongst men,* that *all are upon an equality,* and that the only legitimate right to govern is an express grant of power from the governed. .......
It is the part of wisdom for a republic to limit the service of that officer, at least, to whom she has entrusted the management of her foreign relations, the execution of her laws, and the command of her armies and navies, to a period so short, as to prevent his forgetting *that he is the accountable agent, not the principal—the servant, not the master.* Until an amendment of the constitution can be effected, public opinion may secure the desired object. I give my aid to it by renewing *the pledge heretofore given,* that, under no circumstances, will I consent to serve a second term."

" *The pledge heretofore given,*" is an expression to be particularly observed. Hence it appears that the Presidents, as well as the representatives, give pledges prior to their election ; submit to be interrogated by the electors, as to their opinions and future policy, and even make proposals for the surrender of a part of their official authority. This, doubtless, is to be " the servant, not the master."

But when the British Sovereign ascends the throne of his ancestors, and is crowned with sacred solemnity, he receives his great power and dignify with none other than its constitutional rights and limitations. He may resign the crown, but he cannot abdicate the monarchy. Neither can he extend or limit its prerogatives.

He is our's

T' administer, to guard, t' adorn the state,
But not to warp or change it. We are his,
To serve him nobly in the common cause,
True to the death, but not to be his slaves.

It would be unconstitutional, therefore, and undignified

in the British monarch, to expostulate with his subjects, in long argumentative addresses. It is also unnecessary, because his ministers sit in parliament.

There is an essential difference between the position of the British Sovereign and that of the American President, as regards the connection of each with the legislature; and it is important to observe it narrowly, and to trace its consequences.

By the American constitution, " all the legislative powers are vested in Congress;" and General Harrison remarked, in the address already referred to, that " the President is not a part of the legislative power; and his privilege to *recommend* measures to the legislature, he holds *in common with every other citizen;* the only difference being, that there may be something more of confidence in the propriety of the measures recommended by the President; but in the obligation of ultimate decision there can be no difference." In short, if after he has published his address, or made any other recommendation to the legislature, some citizen should reply to it by a pamphlet, or a letter in the newspapers, and Congress should prefer the recommendations of the citizen to those of the President, they will adopt the one and reject the other.

If the views of the President and his ministers, on any important question, are opposed to those of the majority of Congress, and if the President exercises his veto, an open collision takes place between the executive and the legislature, as in the case of President Tyler's repeated refusals to assent to bills sanctioned by them. Several American statesmen have proposed to alter the constitution, by enabling a bare majority to set aside the President's veto, which would render it almost nugatory, and would practically amount to this, that the bill must be read again in Congress, where the same majorities that passed it before, would generally repeat their former decision, and complete their triumph.

In England the ministers cannot long continue to conduct the affairs of the nation, in opposition to a majority of the house of commons, especially if they are unsupported by a majority of the peers. The legislature does not, as in America, absorb the executive. The relative powers of the estates of the realm are so admirably adjusted, that when they cease to act together in harmony, if a change be not made in their mutual relations, the government cannot be carried on—the machine stops.

It seems paradoxical, but it is *just, because the executive has influence in the legislature,* that the legislature, and through its popular branch, that the *people* can *react* on the executive, so as to determine by *what party, and on what principles,* the country shall be governed.

Before illustrating this beautiful and important result of the practical working of our constitution, I would dispose of an obvious objection to an hereditary monarchy,—namely, that whatever be the age, the sex, or the character of the heir to the throne, there is no deviation from the order of succession. The force of the objection is admitted; but the reply is, that both the conduct of human life and of national affairs often present only a choice of difficulties. The objections to an *elective* monarchy in this country are *insuperable.** The other alternative is an hereditary monarchy, and how are its lesser and incidental evils compensated?

Let it be supposed, that instead of a man of mature age and experience, and of superior talent, the British Sovereign, on succeeding to the throne, should be young and amiable, but inexperienced. In the old

* See page 101.

feudal times, it is probable that one or more powerful
barons would virtually have ruled the kingdom. But
now, the young monarch would be surrounded by the
ministers that were in office at the time of the royal
demise, and must at first be guided by their counsels.
The parliament and the nation would jealously watch
their conduct. Supposing their measures to be impo-
litic and injurious, the Sovereign might be kept in
ignorance of their evil tendency. The just complaints
of faithful statesmen and loyal subjects might seldom
penetrate the guarded avenues of the palace, or might
be represented there as the cry of a faction. Must the
nation hopelessly submit to a long period of misrule?
If the legislature were in the main sound and uncor-
rupted, and the people not besotted and blind to their
real welfare, the remedy would not be long delayed,
and it would be effectual. Parliament would modify
or reject the bad and unconstitutional measures of the
ministers, and forewarn them that their power was on
the wane. Perseverance in their disastrous policy
would involve defeat on some important cabinet question. The voice of the constitution, echoed by the
country, would proclaim and repeat the unwelcome
word, "resign." If deaf to the call, opposing parliamentary majorities would resist their progress, and
compel them to advise the Sovereign to dissolve parliament. The prevailing sentiments of the nation would
then be expressed in a general election, and if that
public verdict were condemnatory of their policy, the
ministers would be forced, however reluctantly, to quit
their places, and surrender their misused power.

The case supposed is not an *improbable* one, though
it may be of rare occurrence in our modern history.
It well illustrates the power of the constitution to rectify
incidental evils. Or if a King, more skilled by age and
experience to govern the empire, should perceive that

his ministers were steering the vessel of the state on a wrong and perilous tack, it would be his prerogative at once to appoint others to take the helm.

What better proof can there be of the admirable manner in which the British monarchy is both upheld and limited by constitutional right and liberty, than the quiet succession, the peaceful and happy reign of our young and beloved Queen?  In any but the best ordered state, how perilous would be the devolution of the sovereignty of an immense empire into the hands of a minor and a female.  But here, the throne, sustained by justice and righteousness, stands firm on the broad and stable foundation of wise institutions, and is guarded by the best affections of a free people.  The coward's villainous attempt to harm the sacred person of his Sovereign, or to hurt her feelings, only serves to display her noble heroism, and to strengthen our attachment the more, while it draws down upon himself a nation's indignant resentment.  Whether she passes through the crowded streets of her capital, or among the mountain wilds of Caledonia, her glad subjects welcome her with chivalrous loyalty and love. The storms of party strife, that sometimes shake the vigorous boughs of our deeply-rooted oak, stir not that slender stem, on which England's queenly rose blooms gracefully, unruffled, and secure.

But dangers may lurk even here, and let us mark from what quarter they are most likely to come.

The two branches of the British legislature check each other by the mutual right of rejecting the bills which originate in either house,—both are influenced, and may be checked by the executive, and the executive is checked by the legislature.  Owing to this admirable contrivance, none of the powers of the state is absolute, and they can only move together and in concert.  While each retains its due share of authority, harmony will be preserved. The parliament will legislate with freedom, and the executive will act with vigour. The executive can only obtain the immense supplies *necessary for carrying on the government,* by means of a vote of the house of commons. Therefore, when ministers cannot command a majority in that assembly, they are powerless, and the King must soon appoint successors who can,—or in other words, whose principles and policy are approved by that majority. The King can only govern through his ministers. To be convinced that the popular branch of the legislature must triumph, in a contest with the executive, we need not go back to the days of Charles I., when the then great and arbitrary power of the monarch was annihilated, and the sceptre was broken by the giant mace of the house of commons; nor even to the time of his popish successor, James II., who was quietly deposed by a great and bloodless and glorious revolution. The events of our own times of greater freedom and tranquillity shew plainly what must be the inevitable result of every such conflict.

The royal veto on the proceedings of parliament has not been exercised since the revolution: the executive could not, by means of the veto, withstand the encroachments of the legislature. The power of the executive mainly consists in the *influence of the crown, exercised through the minister and his adherents in the house of commons.*

Prior to the reform bill it was exercised *directly* by the nomination of a certain number of members to represent treasury boroughs; and *indirectly* by the disposal of the honours and patronage of the crown, which influenced the nomination of other members representing limited constituencies, or attached them to the government. The influence of the crown did *not* enable the cabinet to command an *absolute* majority of the house. When *the great body of representatives* were decidedly opposed to the measures of the cabinet, the measures, if obnoxious to the house and to public opinion, were abandoned, or the ministers were forced to resign. Before matters came to that issue, those proceedings were often modified by the views and opinions elicited by discussion. But when the majority of the house was decidedly with the minister, or when its unbiassed decisions would nearly hang in the balance, those votes on which every minister, at the formation of his cabinet, could depend, almost as certainly as on the votes of the cabinet itself, enabled him to carry through his measures, and to follow out the *general* plan of his government.

This was a very important power, and if wisely, honestly, and ably exercised, it afforded great advantages for the government of our empire, with its complicated and manifold interests, foreign, colonial, and domestic.

There were strong and very effectual checks to the improper use of this power of the minister. For he is generally a commoner, and with his colleagues depends on the Sovereign, the parliament, and the electors, for his continuance in office, and is liable to impeachment for any flagrant abuse of authority; his reputation for wisdom, integrity, and talent, are hourly at stake, in a country where public opinion has the greatest weight, and public men and measures undergo the strictest scrutiny. The house of commons would by itself be incompetent to the conduct of affairs in ordinary times,—how much more so in those emergencies when the utmost dispatch, secresy, and energy, are necessary; when every thing may be marred by wasting time in the endeavour to sway a large and mixed assembly, by the motives and reasons that urge the ministers to a prompt and unanimous decision. At such critical periods, the wisdom, the energy, the judicious, and consistent management of a cabinet of upright and able men, are invaluable. What confidence have the nation felt in times of foreign and domestic trouble, knowing that the strong hand of a minister, in whose integrity and skill they relied, firmly grasped the helm of affairs, that his undaunted eye was directed to the landmarks of our venerated institutions, and the polestar of our safety.

The electoral system was, doubtless, susceptible of much improvement, by transferring the franchise from some of the decayed boroughs to flourishing towns, and by obviating various abuses. Those ameliorations, too long delayed, were introduced by the reform bill, together with other changes, materially affecting the constitution of the legislature and its relations with the executive. It can no longer be truly affirmed "that the power of the crown has increased, is increasing, and ought to be diminished." The constitution has rather been endangered from another quarter,—by a transference of power from the executive to the majority of the house of commons, which at all times can arrest the arm of the executive by causing the dismissal of ministers and effecting a change of policy. The ministers may be of first rate talent, and their plans and proceedings may be wise, comprehensive, and consistent. But when parties are nearly balanced, any particular class, interest, or faction, under an adroit and persevering leader, commanding a certain number of votes in the lower house, may seriously thwart the measures of government. Thus the cabinet, in order to gain the support of some adverse party and retain office, might be tempted to abandon or modify good measures, to concur in injurious ones, and to yield up the constitution, piecemeal, to skilful aggression. The faction thus made stronger by every concession, which weak-

I

ened the executive, might repeat their assaults and
conquer by *instalments.* A dispassionate consideration
of the course of affairs during the last ten or twelve
years may convince us that these dangers are not
imaginary.

When the reform bill passed, the opinion prevailed
that the treasury and nomination boroughs were a
blemish, and they were abolished. Such is now the
constitution, and in tracing its modern history I merely
wish to shew the practical effect of their removal.

Some of the brightest ornaments of the senate and
firmest friends of constitutional freedom, who might
otherwise have been unable to enter parliament, were
returned for close boroughs; and their distinguished
services, formerly unknown to the public, were thus
secured to their country in the prime of their manhood
and their genius. That advantage at least could not
be denied to the nomination boroughs, by the most
fervent hater of Boroughbridge, or of Old Sarum,—

> " Which, like the toad, ugly and venomous,
>   Wore yet a precious jewel in his head."

But now, the prime minister is actually restricted as to
the choice of a cabinet, by the difficulty of finding
seats in parliament for all whom he is desirous to have
as members of his administration. Formerly there was
no such difficulty, and he could also secure the aid of
a few auxiliaries, to strengthen his position against any
faction commanding votes enough to perplex and
defeat the plans of the administration, by turning the
scale when parties were nearly balanced. The legitimate
use of that influence of the minister, in the lower
house, was to render the government superior to
cabals and particular interests,—to enable it to be
energetic, yet not arbitrary. It was a power somewhat
liable to abuse. What power is not? But it was

entrusted to the chosen and responsible servants of the crown. Were it now to fall into the hands of factious leaders, it would be used wrongfully, irresponsibly, and with impunity.

If the preceding remarks have been sufficiently clear, it will be seen, that by the passing of the reform bill, a transference of considerable power has been made from the executive to the popular branch of the legislature, to be exercised by its fluctuating majorities.

Whether the executive shall be able to maintain even its present relative position, must depend on the future constitution of the house of commons. If the legitimate influence of property, character, and intelligence, in the electoral system, shall not be further and excessively diminished, then, through the good sense of the nation, their just ideas of liberty, and their strong and judicious attachment to the national institutions, our limited monarchy may continue to flourish—then the recipro-cal influence of the three great powers of the state may yet be maintained—the executive may continue to act with vigour and the people to enjoy well regulated freedom.

It will tend to so desirable a result, if the old tory and the modern whig shall both abate their prejudices —if men of character and intelligence, to whatever sect or party they belong, shall happily learn to be more tolerant of each other, by respecting the rights of conscience, and making due allowance for the effect of circumstances and education on the minds of other men. Thus, without any compromise of truth, or any violation of liberty, Christian charity and mutual for-bearance may subdue those discordant, imperious, and hostile feelings, by the indulgence of which, the permanent safety, peace, and happiness, of all, must be sacrificed to the bigotry of a few.

If, on the contrary, the parliamentary constituencies

shall become more and more democratic, and shall impart a republican character to the house of commons —if the ballot, and short parliaments, and a widely extended or universal suffrage, shall make the power of numbers paramount to the influence of property, character, and intelligence, the consequences are plainly indicated by the theory of our constitution, by the history of England and of the United States,—and by the signs of these eventful times. Men of talent would in that case be systematically excluded from parliament, and men of inferior abilities and attainments, and of republican principles, would constitute the popular branch of the legislature, and thus engross nearly the whole power of the state. The executive would retain only the shadow and semblance of authority. This has already come to pass in America, but under peculiarly favourable circumstances, and without having yet caused the full measure of evil which may be expected to ensue from it hereafter. Such a change in England would be a tremendous revolution,—with our immense metropolis, our crowded mercantile cities, and manufacturing districts,—power, in the hands of the multitude, would be set in hostile array against property and rank, the artificer and labourer against their employers, the inferior minds of the community against the superior,—might against right.

Montesquieu, after his well known eulogy of the British constitution, as the most perfect of all forms of government, predicts from what quarter it will receive its fatal blow:—"As all human things have an end, the state we are speaking of will lose its liberty—it will perish. Have not Rome, Sparta, and Carthage, perished? It will perish when the legislative power shall be more corrupted than the executive." In other words, it will perish when the legislature shall be basely seduced or blindly impelled to abuse its great power for the overthrow of the monarchy.

May the Almighty, who has so often preserved us in the hour of danger, avert from our beloved country the doom of fallen nations. Sparta, Rome, Carthage, were heathen—England is a Christian country. Let that salt of the earth—pure preserving Christianity—be diffused throughout the mass of our population, and ours will be the righteousness which exalteth a nation, and saveth it from ruin; "but if the salt have lost his savour, wherewith shall it be salted?"

The most distinguished founders of the American constitution foresaw that it was threatened with danger in the same direction. General Hamilton spoke of the almost irresistible tendency, in republican governments, of the legislative authority to absorb every other. He doubted whether the President's position, with an office of only four years' duration, or for any other limited period, would completely answer the end proposed; although the American executive was energetic, "as far as republican principles will admit." Jefferson informs us, that General Hamilton considered the " British constitution, with all the corruptions of its administration, to be *the most perfect model of government that had ever been devised by the art of man.*" While of the government of the United States he said, " It is not that which will answer the ends of society, by giving stability and protection to its rights, and it will probably be found expedient *to go into the British form.*"—JEFFERSON's *Memoirs.*

Quite similar was the opinion of the great Washington, for Jefferson also tells us, " I do believe that General Washington had not a firm confidence in the durability of our government. Washington was influenced by the belief, that we must at length end *in something like a British constitution.*"—And is it possible, that while such were the opinions of the two ablest American statesmen, there are Englishmen so infatuated as to endeavour to make the British constitution END in something like an American one ?— " He has often declared to me, that he considered our new constitution as an experiment on the practicability of republican government, and with what *dose* of liberty man could be trusted for his own good." Washington, as a wise physician, knew that an *over dose* of that deliciously intoxicating medicine might prove noxious and even deadly. The candid confessions of a democrat would be not less instructive than those of " an opium eater."

The world did not elsewhere afford so fair and ample a field as North America, for trying that bold experiment, under the most favourable circumstances. Jefferson well knew that these advantages were peculiar to America, and sanguine as that ardent republican was, at one period, as to the success of the grand experiment in the United States, he did not commit the blunder of supposing that it could succeed in the states of Europe. " A government adapted for which (he says) would be one thing; but a very different one that for the men of these states. Here in America, every man may have land, to labour for himself, if he chooses ; or preferring the exercise of any other industry, may exact for it such compensation as not only to afford a comfortable subsistence, but wherewith to provide for a cessation of labour in old age." But he sees a period to the continuance of tranquillity, after the vacant lands shall have been occupied ; " *when we get piled upon one another in large cities, as in Europe,* we shall become corrupt, as in Europe, and go to eating one another, as they do there."

At a later period of his life, Jefferson appears to have discovered, as most men do by sad experience, that the selfishness and passions of mankind are not to be curbed by reason and argument alone; and that to commit to the fickle multitude the task of governing themselves, is to give them up to misrule.—"I envy not the present generation the glory of throwing away the fruits of their fathers' sacrifices of life and fortune, and of rendering desperate the experiment, which was to decide ultimately whether man is capable of self-government. ...... I regret that I am now to die in the belief, that the useless sacrifice of themselves, by the generation of 1776, to acquire self-government and happiness to their country, is to be thrown away by the unwise and unworthy passions of their sons; and that my only consolation is to be, that I live not to weep over it."— JEFFERSON's *Memoirs*, Vol. IV. pp. 331, 333.

It was, indeed, an experiment, for history does not afford a single example of a great nation having continued to flourish as a republic. The United States are a confederacy of small republics, and they remain united, not so much by the controuling power of their federal government, as by the natural cohesion of place and circumstances.

With reference to the period at which he expressed it, the following opinion of President Adams regarding the American constitution, is one in which we may safely concur. In a letter to a friend he wrote:— "Our own constitution I have represented as the best for us, in our peculiar situation. I have represented the British constitution as *the most perfect model that has yet been discovered or invented by human genius and experience, for the government of the great nations of Europe.—It is a masterpiece.* It is the *only system* that has preserved the shadow, the colour, or the semblance of liberty to the people, in any of the great nations of Europe." — *Letter to* S. PERLEY, *June,* 1809.

Such is the unbiassed testimony of the most celebrated American statesmen, who, in their ardent love
of liberty, striving to found the most perfect form of
government in a new country, took our constitution for
their pattern, and, having narrowly examined its excel-
lencies and defects, pronounced it to be an unrivalled
masterpiece.

By their verdict let us contentedly and gratefully
abide; and perhaps the best advice that can be offered
to those whose democratic propensities are too strong
to be satisfied with liberty, in the most perfect form in
which it has ever appeared upon earth, is, that they
should hie them away to America, where they will find
a constitution the best for them, "in their peculiar
situation," and with their peculiar opinions.

From the preceding investigation, it appears that the
British empire, with its colonies, cannot be governed,
either as a simple or a confederated republic.—That to
give a democratic character to our electoral system, and
consequently to the house of commons, would weaken
or annul the executive. — That the subversion of the
monarchy would involve the dissolution of the empire.

The Abyssinian traveller, Bruce, when he had attained the object of his toilsome and dangerous journies,
by the discovery in the desert of the original fountain
of the great river that fertilises Egypt, is said to have
gazed on it with inexpressible emotion. In one of the
most crowded thoroughfares of London, is a spot but
little heeded by the busy passengers, that might suggest
far more striking and useful reflections than the source
of the famous Nile. On one side of the way is White-
hall palace, where a republican axe felled the discrowned
head of Charles the First; on the other, are some un-
attractive buildings, where the officers of state of the
restored British monarchy transact its great affairs,
without pomp or shew, but with unexampled vigour.

*There* is the source of a power, which flows forth to the ends of the earth. That power is acknowledged from the presidencies of Bombay, Madras, and Calcutta, to the banks of the Indus, by Mahommedan and Hindoo races and princedoms of the east. It rules over the liberated negroes of Africa and the West Indies, and the free settlers of the fine provinces of Canada, New Brunswick, and Nova Scotia, in the American continent. It has military and commercial stations, and colonial settlements, at Gibraltar, Malta, and the Ionian islands, in the Mediterranean and the Levant, at St. Helena, at the Falkland isles, near remote Cape Horn, at Halifax and Bermuda, on both extremities of the North American coast, on the shores of New Holland, Van Dieman's Land, New Zealand, at Ceylon, Penang, Singapore, Malacca, and on the coasts and rivers of the formerly inaccessible Chinese empire.

In manufacturing industry Great Britain is unequalled; on her prosperity depends that of the commercial world; her reverses are felt, as when the sun withdraws its beams, and the clouds withhold their moisture. For what harbour is unvisited by her fleets, what mart is not supplied by her merchandise? In her wide dominions there is not a slave; and it is her noble and beneficent policy to give liberty to the captive, and a refuge to the oppressed.

In the loftiest and most useful discoveries of art and science, in sound learning and elegant literature, in refinement of manners, in all that enlightens and humanizes mankind, our country is eminently and happily distinguished. She has been the honoured instrument of circulating the holy scriptures, that the nations may read in their own tongues the wonderful works of God; and on savage shores, before unvisited by the enterprising merchant, the more enterprising missionary of the gospel has prepared his way.

When was such extensive authority so tempered with justice and mercy? when was so great power in the ruler, combined with so much liberty in the subject?

From this island throne, Britons can look forth to the far limits of an empire, greater than that which the eastern monarch surveyed from the palace of his Babylon. Let us not be unmindful of its humbled origin, and its gradual advancement, through many a doubtful struggle and arduous conflict; let us not forget our national transgressions and unnumbered mercies; 'nor behold our country's present grandeur and exaltation with presumptuous pride, lest the sentence should go forth against her, "The kingdom is departed from thee!" "Let not the wise man glory in his wisdom, neither let the mighty man glory in his might; let not the rich man glory in his riches: but let him that glorieth glory in this, that he understandeth and knoweth me, that I am the Lord which exercise lovingkindness and righteousness in the earth."

If pride, luxury, vice, irreligion—if rebellious discontent and insubordination prey upon the vitals of a state, its dismemberment will speedily follow. Thus other nations have fallen from the summit of their power and glory; and the mightiest kingdom must avoid their errors, in order to escape their doom. Conqueror—Civilizer—Liberator—Evangelist—our Country! may the KING of kings defend thee!

# LAW—RELIGION.

## LECTURE V.

Judicial institutions of England adopted by the Americans—
Juries—Independence of judges—The supreme court of
the United States — Can the religious instruction of a
country be adequately provided for without an established
church ?—Illustrations from England and America.

In the two former lectures, the legislative assemblies
and the executive power of England and of America
have come under review ; and we have next to consider
the administration of justice in both countries.   But
as the admirable judicial institutions and the laws of
England have been adopted by the Americans, with
little alteration, this part of the subject will not detain
us long.

The most striking and essential feature of the administration of justice in England, is its entire separation from the legislative and executive powers of the
state.   The combination of the judicial power with
either of them is fatal to liberty, and constitutes those
forms of tyranny which, in various degrees, exist elsewhere.   We hear and we read of secret accusations,
dropped into the lion's mouth at Venice, by some hidden blood-thirsty foe; of the dungeons of that city; of
the inquisition and the bastile; of the revolutionary

guillotine, the Russian knout, the Turkish bowstring, and the slave driver's lash, as things horrible, most strange, and inconceivable to ourselves.   For in these happy islands, stealthy deliberation on the doom of untried innocence is unknown, the oppressor's wrong seldom goes unpunished, and justice is glorious in her purity, open as the day, and unconfined as the air of heaven.   It has been observed that the grand object of the whole machinery of our constitution is to uphold, in their integrity and independence, the courts of law at Westminster; and conversely it may be said, that the constitution owes its preservation to the perfection of our judicial system.   It is sufficient to advert to the well known safeguards, by which every man guiltless of crimes is enabled to walk abroad in conscious freedom and security, and not only to view the court of justice and the gaol without dismay, but to hail them as bulwarks of his own and his country's liberty,—a terror only to evil doers, the protection of those that do well. In England a man may not be arrested and imprisoned without the warrant of a magistrate, and if wrongfully imprisoned he will obtain complete redress.   If honest and respectable, he may always procure bail.   The Habeas Corpus act prevents long and oppressive detention in prison.   The grand jury must find a true bill against the accused party, before he can be tried; and trial by jury and the independence of the judges secure the acquittal of the innocent.   All our judicial institutions and proceedings incline in favour of the accused; and although for this reason not a few of the guilty may escape merited punishment, we gladly tolerate an inevitable imperfection, which proves how carefully the laws protect all those that honestly obey them.

Trial by jury affords us the same kind of protection in questions affecting property, that it does regarding

liberty and life, with this important and valuable difference, that whereas the acquittal of a jury absolves a
man for ever from the same criminal charge; in civil
cases, the judge may refuse to receive an erroneous
verdict, and may order a new trial, when the substantial ends of justice require it.

One of the finest spectacles which our country affords
is an intelligent jury, chosen by the regular forms of
law, that are necessary to secure strict impartiality,
and taking their seats, bound by the sacred solemnity
of an oath, to judge in their neighbours' cause as they
would themselves be judged. No other institution is
better calculated not only to maintain order, equity,
freedom, and right, but also to diffuse the knowledge
and to inspire the love of these great principles.

So deservedly dear, to Englishmen, are these admirable institutions, that, wheresoever their descendants
have settled in foreign lands, they have been carefully
established and preserved. We have only, therefore,
to note a few points in comparing the administration
of justice in England and the United States.

"In America," says M. De Tocqueville, "all the
citizens, who exercise the elective franchise, have the
right of serving upon a jury. The great state of New
York, however, has made a slight difference between
the two privileges, but in a spirit quite contrary to that
of the laws of France, for, in the state of New York,
there are fewer persons eligible as jurymen than there
are electors. It may be said in general, that the right
of forming part of a jury, like the right of electing
representatives, is open to all the citizens; the exercise
of this right, however, is not put indiscriminately into
any hands. Every year a body of municipal or county
magistrates,—called *select men*, in New England;
*supervisors*, in New York; *trustees*, in Ohio; and
*sheriffs of the parish*, in Louisiana,—choose for each

county a certain number of citizens, who have the
right of serving as jurymen, and who are supposed to
be capable of exercising their functions. These magistrates, being themselves elective, excite no distrust;
their powers, like those of most republican magistrates,
are very extensive and very arbitrary, and they frequently make use of them to remove unworthy or incompetent jurymen. The names of the jurymen, thus
chosen, are transmitted to the county court; and the
jury, who have to decide any affair, are drawn by lot
from the whole list of names."

Here our and their systems do not essentially differ.
It is necessary that the office of juryman, which is,
in fact, a judicial office, should devolve only on
individuals that are competent by intelligence, integrity, and independence, to exercise it; and, in both
England and America, probably sufficient care is
taken to secure that result. Certainly, in England,
none of us would deem our liberties more secure, and
expect to find justice better administered, were the
office to descend lower, and become, as some would
have the suffrage to be,—universal.

In England, the independence of the judges is
secured by the statute 1st George III., c. 23, which
was enacted at the earnest recommendation of his
Majesty, soon after his accession to the throne, who
declared that " he looked upon the independence and
uprightness of the judges as essential to the impartial
administration of justice ; as one of the best securities
of the rights and liberties of his subjects; and as most
conducive to the honour of the crown." The English
judges are appointed by the crown, but hold their
offices permanently; their full salaries are secured to
them, and they can only be removed for misconduct,
on the address of both houses of parliament. From the
following remarks of M. De Tocqueville, it appears

that the same independence is not universally secured to the judges of the United States.—" I am aware that a secret tendency to diminish the judicial power exists in the United States; and, by most of the constitutions of the several states, the government can, upon the demand of the houses of the legislature, remove the judges from their station. By some other constitutions the members of the tribunals are elected, and *they are even subjected to frequent re-elections.* I venture to predict that these innovations will, sooner or later, be attended with *fatal consequences;* and that it will be found out at some future period, that the attack which is made upon the judicial power *has affected the democratic republic itself."*

The supreme court of the United States is an institution to which the union principally owes its permanence. It consists of seven judges, appointed by the President, and removable only by impeachment.

It is to be remembered, that while the control of the general interests of the union is exercised by the federal government, each state is the guardian of its own interests, and has its own courts of law. To have submitted the interpretation of the fundamental laws of the union to these various tribunals, would have given rise to a collision of jurisdiction, which would have caused great inconvenience and disorder. The federal government has, therefore, a court whose constitution is judicial; but its prerogatives are chiefly political. It is the court of the union appointed to execute its laws, and interpret the written constitution, and it has jurisdiction, with regard to the relations of the nation with foreign powers, of the government with the citizens, and of the states with each other. It decides also in maritime causes, and in those arising between the citizens of different states—and between a state and the citizens of *another* state. Questions between

fellow citizens of the same state are almost exclusively
tried before its own tribunals.

The whole union is divided into districts, in each of
which a federal judge resides; and his court is named
a 'district court.' The supreme federal court, consisting
of the seven judges, holds its session at Washington.
It has original jurisdiction in a few cases, but its chief
business is the trial of appeals from the circuit courts,
which are held in the different states twice a year.
Causes before the state courts, in which *any point of
constitutional law* arises, may be brought under the
review of the supreme federal court, which may affirm
or reverse their decisions. But in the *case of reversal*
the superior court's decision is not absolutely final, as
in the British house of lords, but a mandate is issued
to the state court, directing it to conform its judgment
to that of the supreme court. To that important
tribunal, therefore, all questions concerning the proper
interpretation of the written constitution of the United
States must be submitted.

But in America, the constitution binds the legisla-
lature as well as the citizens. It may be altered by
the will of the people in certain specified cases, and
according to established rules; yet, as a constitutional
code, it is the supreme law. The American judges,
consequently, obey the constitution rather than any
enactment of the legislature; and they may, and often
do, refuse to apply such laws as appear to them to be
inconsistent with the constitution. This gives them
immense political influence, and the manner in which
they exercise it has been very skilfully arranged by the
lawgivers who framed the constitution.

The judge is not at liberty to step out of his sphere,
and, of his own act to point out an inconsistency between any law and the constitution. He does so only
when a special case is brought before him. This will

happen when the evil consequences of any enactment are experienced. The judge tries the cause, most commonly, as affecting the interests of a private individual; he finds the law to be unconstitutional, and he decides in conformity with the constitution, and, as if the law had never been enacted, thus silently passing sentence against that measure of the legislature and correcting its error. The law is not by this means abolished; but it cannot be enforced, and if the decision is confirmed on future occasions, it must eventually be repealed. This power of the supreme judiciary forms a valuable and really effectual check to the errors and inconsistencies of the legislative assemblies of the union. The judges have usually had a high reputation for integrity and talent; the decisions of the supreme court are received with much respect, and they tend essentially to harmonize the otherwise discordant elements of the confederation.

" In the nations of Europe," says M. De Tocqueville, " the courts of justice are only called upon to try the controversies of private individuals, but the supreme court of the United States summons sovereign powers to its bar. When the clerk of the court advances on the step of the tribunal, and simply says, 'The state of New York versus the state of Ohio,' it is impossible not to feel that the court which he addresses is no ordinary body; and when it is recollected that one of these parties represents one million, and the other, two millions of men, one is struck by the responsibility of the seven judges, whose decision is about to satisfy or to disappoint so large a number of their fellow-citizens. *The peace, the prosperity, and the very existence of the union are vested in the hands of the seven judges.* Without their active co-operation the constitution would be a dead letter: the executive appeals to them for assistance against the encroach-

K

ments of the legislative powers; the legislature demands
their protection from the designs of the executive ; they
defend the union from the disobedience of the states,
the states from the exaggerated claims of the union,
the public interest against the claims of private citizens,
and the conservative spirit of order against the fleeting
innovations of democracy.   Their power is enormous,
but it is clothed in the authority of public opinion.
They are the all-powerful guardians of a people which
respects law ;  but they would be impotent against
popular neglect or popular contempt.   The force of
public opinion is the most intractable of agents, because
its exact limits cannot be defined : and it is not less
dangerous to exceed, than to remain below the boundary
prescribed.   The federal judges must not only be good
citizens, and men possessed of that information and integrity which are indispensable to magistrates, but they
must be statesmen,—politicians, not unread in the signs
of the times, not afraid to brave the obstacles which can
be subdued, nor slow to turn aside such encroaching
elements as may threaten the supremacy of the union,
and the obedience which is due to the laws.   The
President, who exercises a limited power, may err
without causing great mischief in the state.   Congress
may decide amiss without destroying the union, because
the electoral body in which Congress originates may
cause it to retract its decision by changing its members.
But if the supreme court is ever composed of *impru-
dent men or bad citizens, the union may be plunged
into anarchy or civil war.*   The real cause of this
danger, however, does not lie in the constitution of the
tribunal, but *in the very nature of federal governments.*"

The English judges have no power to dispense
with an act of parliament, on the plea that it is unconstitutional.   The three estates of the realm, whose con-

currence is necessary to the enactment of a law, is necessary also to its modification or repeal.

The next branch of the subject cannot be discussed before a mixed assembly, without stating views and opinions, from which some will differ, who, in the main, may have agreed with the preceding remarks; yet, if the comparison between the British and American constitutions, as respects the religious instruction of the people, be made with a love at once of truth and of charity,—avoiding controversy on questions purely theological, (which here, I admit, would be out of place,) and asking for no verdict that is not warranted by facts, such a statement, I trust, will be received, as it is made, with candour and good will. Here we are to consider the subject as a constitutional, not as a theological question. An integral part of the British constitution is a national and protestant church, to give religious instruction to the *people generally*. All are invited to profit by its ministrations,—while those who dissent from its doctrines or discipline, are free to choose or provide for themselves another mode of worship and instruction.

Undoubtedly the paramount object to be aimed at is, that all the people should become Christians, not in name only, but in deed and in truth. For, how little can the human lawgiver do, without the aid of religion, to inspire men with a reverence for truth and justice, to inculcate pure morality from the highest motives, and to prevent crime. But, for this end, it is not enough that churches and chapels,—comparatively few, in the midst of a numerous and increasing population, —should be built, by those, and for those only, that are *willing* to worship there; while many thousands besides, who profess and call themselves Christians, seldom enter a church or chapel, from the hour of their baptism till that of their funeral. The great

truths of Christianity have been regularly taught in
England for centuries, and in the United States from
its first colonization; consequently there are in both
countries many who are willing to build and endow
places of worship. But the assertion, that the duty of
providing religious instruction for the people may best
be left to their own voluntary zeal and benevolence,—
how far is it borne out by facts ?

Dr. Chalmers, in his Lectures on Church Establishments, which are characterized by that comprehensive
practical wisdom and liberality of sentiment, for which
he is distinguished, says: "If we wait till the taught
seek after the teacher, we shall have to wait for ever;
for, in reference to the great mass and majority of an
alienated parish, there is no taste, no predisposition
for the lessons of the gospel, and nothing, therefore, to
*originate* a right impulse among the people. The only
thing which remains then is, that the teacher shall seek
after the taught. The missionary spirit, or the missionary effort, is required for *short* as well as *long* distances
to reclaim a parish, as well as to reclaim a continent; and
never, but by a system of aggression on the households
of any given territory, shall we be able to retain, and
far less to recover, a parochial congregation."

If all Christians were really united, as Christianity
and truth are one, the territorial or parochial system,
which Dr. Chalmers considers to be the only effectual
method of Christianizing the people, might be carried
into full effect by the state, under one uniform plan,
embracing all its subjects. But, although the truth is
one and perfect, the numerous recipients of it have
manifold errors and imperfections, and hence the
sectarian differences existing within the districts into
which the country is divided for the purposes of
Christian instruction. It is obviously impossible to
allot a distinct territory to each sect.

Dr. Chalmers then supposes that government should abandon the system of parochial division, and endow every sect "within the limits of scriptural and evangelical protestantism;" and he asks, What then would become of those who "choose to be nothing at all?" These would be left in their native irreligion, neglected by the ministers of all sects, as belonging to none. It is obvious, from the experience both of Great Britain, since its parishes became too populous for exact clerical superintendence, and of America, when it had endowed ministers of various denominations, that the community would rapidly degenerate under such a system. In short, the plan of endowing not only all existing but all future sects equally, and of thus providing for the religious instruction and clerical superintendence of the whole people, is utterly impracticable. The state can only perform its duty of promoting the Christian religion by one simple and efficient plan, like that which is recognised by the law and constitution of this protestant kingdom. Its worship and ordinances are celebrated, its doctrines and precepts are taught by a church which takes revelation for her guide. The great body of dissenters agree with the church in those grand truths which lie at the very foundation of religion and morality, and on which our hopes of salvation mainly depend. Thus, not only individually, and by separate classes, but as a nation, we acknowledge the Supreme Being; while our rulers, as the heads and representatives of the nation, may extend to all ranks the benefit of religious instruction. A perfect system may be desired, but a more perfect one cannot easily be obtained.

Dr. Chalmers truly observes, that it is neither to exalt one sect nor to stigmatize others, that government performs its duty, of giving sound religious instruction to the people, by the ministers of one denomination

who "*are vitally and essentially right*," but because
it is thus only that the great object of general Christian
education can be best accomplished. On this broad
and intelligible ground he contends for the necessity of
a national church.

In London, and other large cities, and in many
rural and manufacturing districts, the people have
immensely outnumbered all the means of religious
instruction, whether in churches or dissenting places
of worship. Even in this wealthy Christian country,
the result of throwing the people on their resources,
and leaving them to their own inclinations has been,
that in many towns and districts, not *one tenth,* and
sometimes not *one fifteenth,* or *one twentieth part* of
the inhabitants attend any place of worship; and the
voluntary contributions of the beneficent, to supply
the melancholy deficiency, have not even kept pace
with the increase of the population, amounting to
nearly four hundred thousand souls every year. These
contributions, inadequate as they are, have been chiefly
derived from the middling classes, on whom the burden
falls, with a very unequal pressure; whereas, if it were
generally distributed over the community in proportion
to wealth, it might easily be borne, and the devout
and bountiful would still have ample scope for their
private munificence. Hence a numerous population,
nominally Christian, but practically the reverse, have
sprung up and are multiplying around us. If the
voluntary principle were a sound principle, it would
have proved its efficiency with regard to those unenlightened myriads—those many sheep without a
shepherd.

In republican America, where labour is abundant
and almost all the people are able, if willing, to provide
for their own religious instruction, and where there is
no national church, of which it can even be alleged that

it interferes, directly or indirectly, with spontaneous exertion, how has this voluntary principle proved its vaunted excellence ? The author of " Essays on the Church, by a Layman," has given, in the fifth chapter of his clear and able work, a summary of unexceptionable evidence, derived from the reports of American religious societies, from which I cull a few facts.

A report of the Massachusetts Society for Promoting Christian Knowledge states, that in the counties of Rockingham and Strafford there are forty-five towns, containing upwards of forty thousand inhabitants, which have been destitute of the means of grace, some ten, some twenty, some thirty, some forty years ; and in one town, containing one thousand and sixty-three souls, the visible church of Christ, after *a stated ministry of twenty-eight years,* has been *many years wholly extinct.* In a report, dated 1834, referring to the Baptist churches, it is said, that in the west there are more than *a thousand towns and villages in which there is no stated worship.* The American Tract Society's report for 1833 says, " It is estimated by those who have the best means of judging, that not far from *five millions* of our population are now unblessed with the means of grace." The American Baptist Home Missionary Society's report for 1833 stated, that even if all who profess to be Christian teachers were duly qualified, there would then have been a deficiency of four thousand ministers, to meet the wants of the country. But it is added, a further large deduction must be made for those that are propagating error, —for those who are " *too ignorant of Christianity to teach its doctrines with advantage to others ;*"—for those who are " necessarily *so engaged in secular occupations,* as to prohibit their devoting time to preparation for much usefulness in the ministry. *These facts evince a great and alarming destitution of Christian instruction.*"

These melancholy statistics account too well for the moral debasement of a portion of the population in England and America; and in both countries, wherever true religion prevails,—and to a great extent, we rejoice to say it does prevail,—its proper fruits are manifested, in strong contrast with the surrounding corruption and degeneracy.

M. De Tocqueville's decisive testimony to the efficacy of religion, as a social curb, is very valuable and very striking. He says, " If the minds of the Americans were free from all trammels, they would very shortly become the most daring innovators and the most implacable disputants in the world. But the revolutionists of America are obliged to profess an outward respect for Christian morality and equity, which does not easily permit them to violate the laws that oppose their designs; nor would they find it easy to surmount the scruples of their partisans, even if they were able to get over their own. Hitherto, no one in the United States has dared to advance the maxim, that every thing may be permitted with a view to the interests of society;— an impious sentiment, which seems to have been invented in an age of freedom, to shelter all future tyrants. Thus whilst the *law* permits the Americans to do what they please, religion prevents them from conceiving and forbids them from committing what is rash and unjust.......... How is it possible that society should escape destruction, if the moral tie be not strengthened in proportion as the political tie is relaxed ? And what can be done with a nation which is its own master, if it be not submissive to the Divine Ruler ?"

Thus religion constitutes the grand counterpoise to the evils of a democratic government; and without that holy bond, the people would break loose in wildest anarchy.

The fluctuating nature of their institutions renders

it scarcely possible to found an established church in the United States. With us the question is not whether we shall *found* a national church, but whether we shall *abandon* the sacred institutions handed down to us by our forefathers, in intimate union with our monarchical government, and thus dislocate and rend asunder the whole constitutional fabric.

The churches of England and Scotland have their tithes and endowments secured to them by law as property; rates are levied for the repair of the ecclesiastical edifices, and, according to the argument of Dr. Chalmers, already quoted, this is not for the purpose of giving pre-eminence to any sect, but to maintain and propagate amongst us the Christian religion. In England a protestant episcopal church, and in Scotland a protestant presbyterian church,—in both the creed of the majority,—have been chosen by the state, as the channels through which the blessings of Christianity may be communicated to all ranks of the people, by means of the influence and wealth which the government can command for any great national object.

Confining our view to this part of the United Kingdom, and bearing in mind the religious and moral statistics already adverted to, their result is thus stated, in an important official document—the Second Report of the Ecclesiastical Commission, of which Lord Melbourne and Lord John Russell were members. " The growth of the population has been so rapid, as to outrun the means possessed by the establishment of meeting its spiritual wants: and the result has been, that a *vast proportion* of the people are left destitute of the opportunities of public worship and Christian instruction, *even when every allowance is made for the exertions of those religious bodies which are not in connexion with the established church.*"

The preceding argument has not been given as embracing all the points of this much agitated question, but as that which appears the most proper and essential to be stated on this occasion, and it stands thus.—As Christians and as protestants, we *agree* that the people ought *all* to be instructed in the great truths of Christianity. In England, where there is a national church, not supplied by the government with adequate resources to provide for the spiritual wants of a numerous and often poor population, multitudes are without the means of religious instruction. In America, where there is little poverty, but no national church, the want of religious instruction is still more striking.

A great nation can only be thoroughly Christianized, by a system of parochial visitation and instruction pervading the unenlightened masses of the people.

It would not only be unconstitutional, it would also be impracticable for the British government to attempt to encourage with equal endowments, Christians and Jews, protestants and Roman catholics, pure Christianity and its grossest corruptions, primitive Christianity and the heresies and fanaticism of yesterday.

One denomination of protestant Christians is rightly employed to impart to the people generally the inestimable blessings of our common religion.

To this a dissenter may object—it is all very well for you, a member of the church of England, thus to argue; but why should I be required to contribute to the extension of Christianity, by means of a church from which I dissent?

If the government of England, instead of having chosen the episcopalian, which is the creed of the majority, had selected the independent, or the baptist, or the Wesleyan denomination, as the national church of England, although as an episcopalian I should more or less differ from each of those sects *theologically*, yet, as a *British subject*, I should still concur in the propriety and necessity of a national church, to instruct the multitudes who would otherwise be neglected. According to my particular views, the government might not have made the best selection, but according to the present argument, they would have done far better than if they had made no selection at all. For truly the question is not whether the church of England should prevail over dissent, but whether Christianity should prevail over error, irreligion, and vice.

You object to episcopacy and a liturgy; do you likewise object to the improvement of public morals, and the salvation of your fellow countrymen?

In this free country, and with a protestant church, we all have liberty of conscience. But our Christian liberty surely does not require that millions of our weak and ignorant brethren should *perish*.

When we learn how abundantly the missionary labours of the church societies have been blessed in our colonies and elsewhere, and how wonderfully those of that admirable and devoted man, the martyred Williams, were prospered among the savage islanders of the South Seas, is there a Christian who does not rejoice in such triumphs? Is there a Christian who would deliberately utter such a sentiment as the following: " Doubtless these South Sea islanders have been converted to Christianity, but they are baptists or independents, and I am a churchman; therefore I had rather that the South Sea islanders had continued in their idolatry?" or such a sentiment as this, " The New Zealanders have embraced Christianity, but they have joined the church of England; I am a dissenter, and would therefore have preferred that they had remained heathen?"

If such were our Christianity, surely we should deserve the rebuke of our Divine Lord and Master, " Ye know not what manner of spirit ye are of." How dif-

ferent were such a spirit from that of the zealous and
devoted apostle who said, " Some indeed preach Christ
of envy and strife, and some also of good-will. What
then ? Notwithstanding, every way, whether in pre-
tence or in truth, Christ is preached, and I therein do
rejoice, yea, and will rejoice." (Phil. i.) And are the
thousands who are living or dying around us, ignorant
or regardless of the merciful invitations of the gospel,—
are they less to be pitied by their fellow-countrymen
and neighbours than the far distant heathen ? Have
we indeed resolved to leave *them* in the depths of their
native ignorance and depravity unheeded, and so to let
them perish, because we, who do agree in those grand and
most essential truths whereby they might be saved, are
disputing the while about points and varieties of doctrine, and discipline, and ceremony, that are relatively
less important ?

If this be a correct view of the matter, does not the
question present itself to every Christian in this solemn
form—shall I, a British subject and a professed believer
in the infinite value of the Christian religion, help to
overthrow the established church, which if duly upheld, might bring that religion to every poor and ignorant man's door ? Shall I venture to place obstacles
in the way of those general and public arrangements,
by which religious knowledge may be spread throughout the British isles, and fancy that I am doing God
service ? What scruples of mine, regarding the worship
and the pastoral instruction of the church, can justify
me in acting as if her ministrations were a greater curse
than ignorance and unbelief ? Is not her liturgy, are
not her articles scriptural ? and if the teaching of *all*
her ministers be not so, they are but men; and where,
O where, shall we find perfection ? The variegated
forms and hues of dissent show too plainly how prone our
frail humanity is to depart from a perfect rule of doctrine

and of duty. One calm and sober view of the eccentricities of faith, judgment, and feeling, even among those professing to take revelation for their guide, is enough surely to show candid and reflecting men what need there is of humility, forbearance, charity; to lead all such to rejoice that a church, which they must admit has the main body of the truth, is making her way through the land, and overcoming sin and error in their strongholds. Thus far at least the friends of truth and enemies of bigotry, persecution, infidelity, and wickedness, have a common cause and the same foes. How can they expect to conquer with the sword of Midian ? How shall they prosper and prevail, except they " hold the faith in the unity of the Spirit and the bond of peace ?"

A principal objection to the national church has been well answered by the Rev. H. M$^c$Neile. " We deny that any dissenter is compelled to support our religion. He is compelled to pay tithes and rates, by which the external machinery of our church is supported, but this is a very different thing from supporting our religion. True, the civil ruler, when he receives the taxes, appropriates a portion of them to the support of the church, but this is *his* act, not the act of the man who pays the tax. This distinction will be made manifest to all, by considering for a moment whether the apostle would have exhorted his Christian brethren to *support idol worship:* on the contrary, an apostolical exhortation is, ' keep yourself from idols.' But we have seen that the apostle *did* exhort his brethren to pay tribute to Cæsar, although Cæsar, when he got it, appropriated a portion of it to the support of idol worship. That was *his* act, not the act of the man who paid the tribute. It would be monstrous to say that every man who pays taxes to a government is responsible for its every act. No ; the subject is responsible to God for the duty of *paying* the tribute, and the government is responsible to God for the duty of *appropriating* that tribute. The government receiving taxes may, in one or more instances, make an erroneous, unjust, and unjustifiable appropriation; but the conscience of the man who pays the taxes is in no way implicated. His pocket is assailed, indeed, but not his conscience. This is a most important distinction, not for the dissenter only, but for *us all.*"—*Lectures on the Established Church.*

Although our wants, affections, and desires, are all roused into activity to ward off the evils of poverty, and on the contrary, are in a great degree opposed to religious impressions, the nation is nevertheless taxed to the amount of several millions annually for the relief of the poor. Is poverty then a greater and more universal evil than sin? Is temporal want more to be dreaded than everlasting ruin? Does our care for the poor extend only to the grave? Shall the nation grant millions annually for poor-houses, food, and clothing, while places of worship, and whatever else relates to our condition as immortal beings, is to be left to the voluntary and therefore precarious support of individuals? In its maintenance of an army and navy, in its provision for the administration of justice, and the general management of our foreign and domestic policy, the interference of the government is felt to be necessary, and the objections of the minority are overruled for the public good. And shall not the authority and resources of the government be employed for an object the best, the noblest, the most essential to our individual and national welfare?

The early nonconformists, as Owen, Howe, and Baxter, men of undoubted piety, zeal, and charity, while they dissented from the established church, on other grounds, admitted its necessity and importance

as a national institution, for the diffusion and maintenance of vital Christianity. With a quotation from
Baxter's beautiful exhortation to the nonconformists of
his day, I shall now conclude.

"If you love the COMMON GOOD OF ENGLAND, do
your best to keep up sound and serious religion in the
public parish churches; and be not guilty of any thing
that shall bring the *chief interest of religion* into
private assemblies of men merely tolerated, if you can
avoid it.  *  *  *  *  *  * Let us, therefore, lose
no possession that we can justly get, nor be guilty of
disgracing the *honest conformists* (or churchmen), *but
do all we can to keep up their reputation for the good
of souls.*"

# SOCIAL INFLUENCE OF POLITICAL INSTITUTIONS.

## LECTURE VI.

The will of the majority—The periodical press—Manners—
Liberty—Slavery.

In the United States the legislative and the executive powers are so dependent on the will of the majority
of the people, that the majority may be said to rule,
which is a democratic but a false principle. The multitude is a capricious and IRRESPONSIBLE master. In
its calmer moods it may follow what is just and lawful,
but it is easily excited, and when roused and impelled by
strong prejudice and passion will commit enormous
wrong, without reason, or pity, or remorse. Where
there is a powerful and enlightened government, which
honestly aims to promote the public welfare, even in
opposition to the will of the majority, mobs are awed
and subdued and their ringleaders are punished. But
it is otherwise when the people have assumed the
sovereignty, and have decreed that their will shall be
paramount. Then they will act not only through their
regular legislative assemblies, but they will sometimes
do what they please, and with impunity, in their
irregular and turbulent meetings, where the dictates of

judgment, and mercy, and conscience, are overborne by temporary feelings, whether right or wrong.

Many examples might be given of this wild exercise of irresponsible power in America. In the year 1812, a Baltimore mob sacked the printing office of a newspaper which opposed the war with England, assaulted one editor and killed another. The offenders were tried, and the jury acquitted them. Thus, through the tyranny of the majority, the liberty of the press was interfered with, innocent blood was shed, and the guilty were set free, in open violation of the laws of the country. There were the riots in New York and Philadelphia, when the houses of the abolitionists, the schools and churches of the black population were destroyed, the public approving or omitting to punish those flagrant enormities. There were similar riots at Cincinnati; and in the less civilized districts, there have been executions by what is called Lynch-law, not unlike the summary executions at the lamp posts of Paris, during the revolution. Miss Martineau, after describing a breach of the peace, which happened during her stay at Boston, and an assault on some of the advocates for the abolition of slavery, mentions that no prosecutions followed. She asked an eminent judge, why, and whether there was not a public prosecutor, who might prosecute for a breach of the peace. "He said, it might be done: but he had given his advice against it. Why? The feeling was so strong against the abolitionists; the rioters were so *respectable* in the city, it was better to let the whole affair pass over without notice." Thus the ordinary safeguards of freedom and innocence are rendered unavailing by the arbitrary will of the people.

M. De Tocqueville truly and beautifully remarks, that men are not fit to be entrusted with unlimited power; "and that omnipotence properly belongs to

L

God alone, because He is also infinitely wise and infinitely just." He considers the main imperfection of the democratic institutions of the United States to arise, not from their weakness, but from their uncontrolled power, and the inadequate securities which exist against tyranny. "In the United States," he says, "when an individual or a party suffers injury, from what quarter can redress be obtained? From public opinion? that is controlled by the majority;—from the legislature? it represents and is subservient to the majority;—from the executive? it is the official instrument of the majority. The soldiers and the militia are a military majority; in trial by jury the same power influences the verdict; and in certain states even the judges are elected by the majority."

" I do not say," he continues, "that tyrannical abuses are frequent in America at present, but I affirm that there is *no effectual security* against them, and that the causes which mitigate arbitrary power are to be found in the *circumstances and manners* of the country more than in its laws."

We might be so infatuated as to adopt so much of the American constitution as to erect among us the tyranny of the majority; but we could not also adopt the " circumstances and manners of the country," which M. De Tocqueville says, are the chief mitigations of that tyranny. If, as Miss Martineau informs us,* many of the American rioters are respectable and well-dressed persons, the circumstances and manners of England would not lead to the same result. Who would feel himself safe, or free, or happy, if the embodied will of the *majority* of the inhabitants of London, or Birmingham, or Bristol, might set aside the statutes, and the decisions of the judges,

---

* Society in America.—Chapter on Allegiance to Law.

dispense with the habeas corpus act, and trial by jury, on the plea of the French anarchists and of Tom Paine, that a majority of men, told by the head, ought to govern? It is marvellous that so irrational a delusion should be gravely supported, as that the highest political wisdom and social virtue reside in the greatest number; —that there is more of both in the mob of West-minster, than in the parliament assembled there;—that the cabinet ought to take no measure without first con-sulting the collective wisdom of those heads that are accustomed to deliberate on the constitutions and the affairs of nations, in the beer shops and gin palaces of Whitechapel and St. Giles's. Yet even the illustrious Burke found it necessary to expose such a fallacy, in the following noble passage.

" Neither in France nor in England has the original or any subsequent compact of the state, expressed or implied, constituted *a majority of men, told by the head,* to be the acting people of their several commu-nities. And I see as little of policy or utility, as there is of right, in laying down a principle that a majority of men, told by the head, are to be considered as the people, and that as such their will is to be law. What policy can there be found in arrangements made in defiance of every political principle ? To enable men to act with the weight and character of a people, and to answer the ends for which they are incorporated into that capacity, we must suppose them (by means imme-diate or consequential) to be in that state of habitual social discipline, in which the wiser, the more expert, and the more opulent *conduct,* and by conducting, *enlighten and protect,* the weaker, the less knowing, and the less provided with the goods of fortune. When the multitude are not under that discipline, they can scarcely be said to be in civil society. Give once a certain constitution of things, which produces a variety of conditions and circumstances in a state; and there is in nature and reason, a principle which, for their own benefit, postpones, not the interest but the *judgment*, of those who are *numero plures*, to those who are *virtute et honore majores.*.........The state of civil society which necessarily generates this aristocracy is a state of nature; and much more truly so than a savage and incoherent mode of life. For man is, by nature, reasonable; and he is never perfectly in his *natural state*, but when he is placed where reason may be best cultivated, and *most predominates. Art is man's nature.* We are as much, at least, in a state of nature in formed manhood, as in immature and helpless infancy. Men, qualified in the manner I have just described, form in nature, as she operates in the common modification of society, the leading, guiding, and governing part. It is the soul to the body, without which the man does not exist. To give, therefore, no more importance in the social order, to such descriptions of men, than that of so many units, is a *horrible usurpation.* When great multitudes act together under that discipline of nature, I recognize the *people.* I acknowledge something that, perhaps, equals, and ought always to guide, the sovereignty of convention. In all things the voice of this grand chorus of national harmony ought to have a mighty and decisive influence. But when you disturb this harmony; when you break up this beautiful order, this array of truth and nature, as well as of habit and prejudice; when you separate the common sort of men from their proper chieftains, so as to form them into an adverse army, I no longer know that venerable object called the *people,* in such a disbanded race of deserters and vagabonds."-*Appeal from the New to the Old Whigs.*

The truth which is here so beautifully explained and expanded by Burke is to be found in a book of

infinitely higher value even than his—expressed with
the weight, the brevity, the wisdom, and authority of
holy writ, "Thou shalt not follow a multitude
to do evil." And the history of the people, to whom
that command was addressed, affords a standing and
most memorable proof of the consequences ensuing
from the violation of it. The Jewish multitude prevailed on their Roman governor to liberate a robber
and crucify the Saviour of the world. "His blood,"
they cried, "be on us and on our children." Then
there fell upon their nation the judgments they had
imprecated;—the unparalleled horrors of the siege of
Jerusalem; the destruction of their city and temple;
war and massacre, and the dispersion of their wandering and afflicted race, who are a living commentary on
the emphatic precept—"Thou shalt not follow a multitude to do evil."

The equality of mankind and the alleged right of the
majority to govern are kindred fallacies, the latter
springing out of the former, and they have ever been
favourite topics with demagogues and agitators. Like
the doctrines of infidels, they are old and worn, but
decked out anew with modern facts and circumstances,
to suit the times.

In the Kentish rebellion, about four hundred years
ago, in the reign of our Henry the Sixth, which was
headed by Jack Cade, an Irishman, Dr. Ball, one of
his followers, harangued many thousands of the rebels
on Blackheath, and took the following rhyme for his
text:—

"When Adam delved and Eve span,
Who was then a gentleman?"

Doubtless all men were equal when there was only one
man; but he was the monarch of an earthly paradise,
which he forfeited, by becoming a rebel against his

heavenly King. Could Dr. Ball, or any of his modern
followers, prove that, when the human family were
driven out to till the blighted earth, there was equality
even in the second generation? Was the murderer
Cain, who was accursed, a fugitive, and a vagabond,
equal to his righteous brother Abel?

Men are equal in their liability to common evils,
rather than in their enjoyment of possessions. Change,
calamity, disease, and death, warn the wealthiest, the
proudest, and the highest, that they must be stripped
of every thing, and return to their original dust. But
throughout the sacred volume which inculcates these
lessons, in conformity with our daily experience, diversities of station, of intelligence, of authority, and of
wealth, are acknowledged. It represents the possessors
of these things as neither originally greater nor finally
happier than their fellow-men; but as stewards responsible to a far higher power, for the use or abuse of the
gifts committed to them. " For unto whomsoever
much is given, of him shall be much required," is a
condition inseparable from moral and accountable agents,
and it involves the commonly neglected consideration that power is not in itself good and desirable,
irrespective of the motives for which it is sought after,
and the way in which it is employed.

Can it be supposed that those who are most eager to
unsettle the established order of things, and to wrest
authority from the more competent hands to which it
has been committed, are themselves sufficiently impressed with the immense importance of the trust they
aspire to? Are their motives selfish or beneficent?
and can they calculate the consequences, perhaps the
irremediable mischief, which would attend the rash experiments and violent changes they propose to make?
They who follow such leaders, would also do well to
reflect, that those miseries will " be on them and on

their children;" and that although, when numbers combine to do evil, men may fail to punish the crowd of conspirators and rebels, a multitude cannot prevail against Omnipotence.

M. De Tocqueville says there is no country in which there is *so little true independence of mind and freedom of discussion, as in America,*—a statement which is confirmed by other travellers, and by Americans themselves.* This is perhaps the most striking example of the tyrannical sway of the majority. Let a man oppose, how conscientiously soever, the prevailing opinions of the people, and he will be slighted by those whom he has failed to convince; he must expect to lose all influence and celebrity, and to undergo a kind of social and political excommunication. Thus truth is often suppressed in deference to popular errors, and the progress of sound knowledge and improvement is hindered.

M. De Tocqueville says he perceives how, under certain laws, democracy may extinguish that *intellectual freedom* which is favoured by the social condition of democracy, so that after having broken through other

* " What makes our communications unprofitable in this country, is the dread of giving offence, now to *the majority*, and now to the fashionable or refined. We speak without force, because *not true to our own convictions.*"-DR. CHANNING.

"Liberty of thought and opinion is strenuously maintained in this proud land, it has become almost a wearisome cant; our speeches and journals—religious and political—are made nauseous by the vapid and vain-glorious reiteration. But does it, after all, characterise any community among us? Is there any one to which a qualified observer shall point and say, *there* opinion is free? On the contrary, is it not a fact, a sad and deplorable fact, that in no land on this earth is the mind more fettered than it is here? That here, what we call public opinion has set up a despotism such as exists no where else?"—*Sober Thoughts on the State of the Times.*—Boston, 1835.

restraints, the human mind may become enslaved to the will of the multitude. " As for me," he says, " I am not the more willing to bow my neck to the yoke, because millions would force me to submit to it." (Part II. Vol. I.)

Flattery of his fellow-citizens, as the ruling power, is a tribute which every writer must pay. And M. De Tocqueville assigns as a reason why there have been so few great writers in the United States, that " literature cannot flourish without freedom of opinion, which *does not exist in America*." But in America, as well as in England, the treasures of British literature tend to elevate the standard of opinion, of intellect, of religion, and morality, and that literature has flourished in a country where opinion is free.

" I consider the people of the United States," says M. De Tocqueville, " as a part of the English nation occupied in the cultivation of the forests of the new world, while the European portion of it, less occupied with the common cares and pursuits of life, is enabled to give itself more to reflection and intellectual advancement." He elsewhere observes, " One cannot conceive any thing so anti-poetical as the life of an American usually is."

The periodical press, by communicating information and discussing topics that are immediately and intensely interesting, greatly contributes to form that public opinion which it undertakes to express; and exercises so much power, that it has been said to constitute a fourth estate of the realm. Stamps and licenses not being required for the American public journals, they are conducted with little or no capital; and there are several thousand newspaper establishments in the United States. Religious newspapers are numerous; and doubtless many of them are useful, especially where other means of diffusing religious knowledge are wanting.

Most of the American editors are imperfectly educated; and not a few, having no character of their own to lose, assail other reputations most recklessly.   There are some honourable exceptions to the generally corrupt and degraded character of the newspaper press, as it is described both by travellers and the Americans themselves.   To discuss political questions well, considerable talent is necessary, but none whatever to traduce and vilify, to misrepresent and calumniate.   Nay, the less talent and the less principle, the more coarsely and scrupulously will that vile task be performed.   These harpies attack the public conduct of statesmen, and invade the domestic retirement of private individuals.

"It is a melancholy truth," said President Jefferson, "that a suppression of the press could not more completely deprive the nation of its benefits, than is done by its abandoned prostitution to falsehood.   Nothing can now be believed which is seen in a newspaper. Truth itself becomes suspicious, by being put into that polluted vehicle..........I will add, that he who never looks into a newspaper, is better informed than he who reads them; as he who knows nothing, is nearer the truth than he whose mind is filled with falsehood and errors."—JEFFERSON's *Memoirs*, Vol. IV.

And the American writer, Mr. Cooper, observes, "In escaping from the tyranny of foreign aristocrats, we have created in our own bosom a tyranny of a character so insupportable, that a change of some sort is getting indispensable to peace."

The New York Herald, which is about the size of the London evening papers, is the most extensively circulated journal in the United States.   Each number costs about a penny, and the editor says he sells about thirty thousand copies daily.   A writer in the Foreign Quarterly Review, for October, 1842, in which the flagrant abuses of the American newspaper press are forcibly exposed, describes the notorious editor of the New York Herald, and relates the circumstances of a trial in which he was convicted for two gross libels on Judge Noah. The court consisted of Judge Kent and two of the city aldermen. That eminent and upright judge thought the offence deserved imprisonment; but it had been contrived that an alderman supposed to be favourable to the editor should sit on the bench, out of his regular order, and in place of one who would have given a more unbiassed decision. By the votes of the two aldermen, the wealthy libeller was condemned to pay a small fine,—in mockery of justice. The parties conniving at his escape dreaded his lash, and his power to injure their prospects as candidates at some future election !

Judge Kent, although prevented from awarding the punishment most justly due, fearlessly delivered the following opinion, which sufficiently condemns the sentence of the majority of the court:—" He could conceive no greater curse to the community, than a paper so cheaply published as to be brought under the eye of every body, and yet dealing in falsehood and scandal *from day to day, as its accustomed occupation:* from the malignity of which no man was free; the columns of which were open to the gossip of every one base enough to act the part of an informer: from the assaults of which *neither age nor sex, nor occupation nor profession was exempt:* which had *its emissaries scattered in the large towns and villages of the whole country,* sending their communications to its columns, like the informations dropped into the lion's mouth in Venice: *disclosing the secrets of the family circle, assailing the most sacred professions, and seeking to bring into contempt the sanctuary of justice itself."*

The newspapers, being the staple literature of the majority, excite them to abuse the power with which they are invested by the American constitution. And among persons of superior education and refinement, some, from their dread of the scurrilous abuse of that portion of the press, shrink from public stations in which they might usefully serve their country; and others, from the same cause, are led to swerve from an upright and honourable course. The newspapers, organs and arbiters of that public opinion whose despotic influence is felt by politicians of every grade, traverse the United States, even in the remotest wilds, in myriads. On they flow incessantly, fretting and foaming, like the bitter and briny surges of an angry sea.

The article in the Foreign Quarterly Review, already referred to, contains various illustrations on this point. The extracts in the subjoined note,\* I have taken

* "To Subscribers.—City subscribers of the Daily Herald, who may want the Sunday edition, without having it served on that day, can be supplied by the carriers on Monday morning."

"Great funeral sermon on the late Dr. Channing.— To-morrow evening, in the church of the Messiah, the Rev. Mr. Bellows will deliver a funeral sermon on the piety, genius, and character of the late William Ellery Channing, D. D.

"As the cause and the occasion of this matter is alike interesting and important to religion, to literature, to piety, and to true christian philosophy, we have made arrangements to report *verbatim* the services and sermon, and to publish them in the Herald, on Friday morning. We now invite the whole world to stand by and witness this intellectual effort of our splendid *corps* of reporters—and we challenge the whole press of New York, for a purse of 100 to 500 dollars, to be given to feed the poor, to meet us fairly, and to ascertain by actual fact what newspaper establishment deserves the highest credit for such enterprises."

"A new movement in our City Politics—Taking the Stump.—We have been expecting, in these latter days, to see some extraordinary and novel features developed in the approaching elections in this city; and, according to present *seriatim* from the leading articles of the New York Herald, of Wednesday, October 12, 1842, which, being

appearances, we shall not be disappointed. We have already described the approaches of Fourierism—but there are other elements beginning to bubble.

" It is now ascertained, beyond the possibility of a doubt, that the end of the world will take place next April, and there is very little doubt but that Joe Smith's end has already come. We have seen extraordinary developments in religion, in philosophy, in finance, in almost every thing of late years; and we now expect to see some most remarkable developments in politics, that shall throw the movements of Mormonism, and Millerism, and Fourierism, completely in the shade.

" It appears that the powerful influence of the independent press is extensively prevailing, and in consequence thereof, the approaching election in this city will be different from any that we have had since the time of the revolution. By the movements now making and to be made, the power and corrupt influence of all cliques, caucuses, secret committees, associations, and clubs of rowdies, loafers, butenders, unionists, and all others, will be gone for ever; and if we could say that the devil and all the joints of his tail had gone with them, we might raise a shout of joy and delight; but, unfortunately, he is here still, and apparently, on a long lease. . . . . . . . . . . . . We go for the stump system, root and branch, we will support all stump candidates, tooth and nail. For nothing can be more demoralizing than the present system. We will advocate the cause of any man who is a stump candidate. We will support Mike Walsh, *with all his indictments on his head,* if he takes the stump; we will support John M'Keon on the same ground, although we do not like him; we will support J. N. Reynolds—yes, and we will go farther, and even support James Watson Webb if he'll take the stump. If Col. Webb will only start for member of Congress on his own hook, and take the stump in the Wall-street, or any other district, we will go for him; and we now call upon him to come out and do so.

" Let this ball be kept rolling. Let us have stumps in the Wall-street district, the Five Point district, the Butt Enders district, and the Indomitable district, and let stumping be the order of the day till the election is over."

a single copy of that leading journal, obtained casually, may be taken as a fair specimen of its taste and talent! As such, they are given without further comment.

"THE BEAUTIFUL AND EXTRAORDINARY RHODE ISLAND SUFFRAGE HEROINE, MRS. PARLIN OF PROVIDENCE.—The beautiful and talented heroine of the suffrage party in Rhode Island, Mrs. Parlin, arrived in the city yesterday. This lady, in conjunction with several other Rhode Island ladies, whose husbands were persecuted by the landholders, was the first to start the great clam bakes, which have created such a tremendous sensation, and kept Rhode Island in a stew all the summer. She, acting as Major General of the female suffrage forces, in connection with her aids, were determined that if they could not make havoc of the land-holders, they would make havoc of the clams and seaholders. She is the wife of a highly respectable physician of Providence, and is the daughter of a respectable New England family, of the Taunton stock.

"It seems that many of these ladies, whose husbands have been persecuted by the landholders, got up a fourth of July celebration on their own hook, had the declaration of independence read, and went through the ceremonies of the day with great *éclat*. This was the first great movement of the women; they have since got up all sorts of clam bakes, and are now going to close the summer campaign, and open the winter with a splendid ball at Pawtucket.

"The lady in question is one of the finest specimens of New England, or Rhode Island beauty. [Here follows a minute description of the lady's personal charms.] Altogether she may be considered a perfect *beau ideal* of Juno, when she set every thing to rights in Olympus, and made all the gods and goddesses mind their p's and q's in the empyrean region. She is here for the purpose of completing the arrangements for the ball, where all the beauty of Rhode Island will be present; and a great number of handsome young democrats from this city, Boston, and all round the country.

"N. B. Tickets for the ball sold at this office; also a full and picturesque history of Rhode Island affairs will be given to-morrow."

"GLORY BY THE OUNCE.—The Pells sold yesterday morning an extensive catalogue of sterling silver plate, including a part of the costly and magnificent service presented to

The following extract from an American newspaper describes a procession at New York, on the anniversary of the day when the British forces quitted the town, called by the Americans " Evacuation day." It is a ludicrous attempt at the sublime.

" Then followed the bold musicians pouring the martial strain from fife and drum and trumpet, giving old winter blast for blast; then came the grim and frowning cannons, two of them,—each with its tumbrel charged with the fiery dust that emulates the vollying thunder; and last, though far from least, the sturdy veterans of the ancient corps, disdaining all the foppery of Mars, and breasting the pitiless north wind and driving sleet—in their plain blue coats.—And so they marched along unmindful of the storm, while the shrill notes of the trumpet struggled through the snow-encumbered air." This may pass muster in the columns of an American newspaper, but it would make sad work in the columns of an army. If a commanding officer were to order his men to "charge their grim muskets with the fiery dust that emulates the vollying thunder, and to breast the pitiless north wind in their plain red coats, unmindful of the storm," the soldiers might fancy he was drilling a regiment in the clouds. But prime and load—march—sets the column in motion in a moment. The Duke

Commodore Stephen Decatur by the city of Baltimore, for one of his brilliant naval victories over the English in the last war. This service of plate was valued at three thousand dollars, and the widow of the gallant commodore was compelled to dispose of it, but not without a pang. Congress had promised her relief, but the petty squabbles of that body prevented any from being granted, and the plate had to go for bread and butter."

"☞ COLONEL DICK JOHNSON is in Philadelphia. Come on to this city, old hero, and let us shake you by the same hard but benevolent hand, that wielded the sword in the battle of the Thames, and helped to lick the British. Do."

of Wellington disdained both the foppery of Mars and the foppery of language, and his few and pithy words in the hour of victory at Waterloo were, " Up, guards, and at them."

It is unnecessary to dwell at any length either on the merits or the abuses of the British periodical press, with which we are so familiar. The principal newspapers of the metropolis are in few hands, and some of them are very valuable property, and are conducted with a high degree of talent. The terse, appropriate, and forcible style in which the leading articles are struck off, from day to day, the accuracy with which the parliamentary debates are reported, the expense and trouble incurred to obtain speedy and correct information from all parts of the globe, the rapidity with which it is arranged, condensed, and published, place the principal journals of London among the most wonderful achievements of modern art and enterprise. Many of our provincial newspapers too are conducted in a style highly creditable to their proprietors and editors.

The low unstamped prints that defraud the revenue, and disseminate sedition and slander, may mislead and corrupt their unwary readers; but they are utterly disregarded by the more respectable part of the community. The rich proprietor of the most extensively circulated Sunday newspaper was rejected as a candidate for the mayoralty of London, in consequence of his connection with a print remarkable for its shameless and indecent disloyalty and profaneness. The better portion of the press use, indeed, great, and sometimes excessive freedom, in animadverting on the conduct of public men; but rarely are they guilty of slandering private character. Neither the verdicts of juries, nor the public voice, would support them in such outrages, the frequent recurrence of which, in any of the principal newspapers, would certainly tend to lessen its repute and its respectable circulation.

While the literary talent employed in the daily press, cultivated as it is by constant practice, is quite remarkable, the habit of discussing every subject on the spur of the moment must often lead to a method of writing which is striking and brilliant rather than just and profound; and mistaken opinions on important questions once adopted may sometimes be defended with ability and ingenuity worthy of a better cause.  Yet truth and freedom are on the whole promoted by free discussion; and if those great organs of information and public opinion occasionally excite feelings that had better remain dormant, they also give vent to those which it would be dangerous to suppress; their warnings and suggestions are useful to the government, and their Argus eyes and trumpet tongues constitute an invaluable check to every abuse.   Surely the advantages of the British press far preponderate over its incidental evils.

We had need, however, to take care that the periodical writing of newspapers, and of the singularly able and spirited articles which appear in our reviews and magazines, be not allowed to provoke harsh and uncharitable sentiments, nor yet implicitly to guide our opinions on vitally important questions.  Those articles must generally be hastily written, they are often highly seasoned, and even where there is no deliberate intention to misrepresent, such a habit of writing is very likely to lead to misrepresentation, not only of the characters and opinions of the parties opposed to the writer, but also of the party whose advocate he is.   A periodical writer will generally be found in the van of his party, and we are far too apt to judge of all parties by the extreme views of their accredited public organs. If we dislike the published sentiments, we are inclined to shun all whom we suppose to hold them; and so to regard one another with hostility, like Jews and Sama-

ritans, or the semi-barbarous clans of ancient Caledonia
and Erin, who transmitted their feuds from father to
son. Yet there are many that range themselves under
hostile banners, who have only to meet on some neutral
ground, and discuss their differences in a friendly spirit,
in order to discover points of agreement and reasons
for mutual forbearance and good-will. By all means
let truth be advocated with the ardour of honest conviction, and let pestilent errors be manfully opposed.
But therefore it is the more necessary, not to suffer
strong prejudice and antipathy to close our hearts
against the common sympathies and interests of our
people and our race. And if party spirit has chilled
the social scene around us, and overspread it with a
severe and wintry aspect, only let Christian charity
shed her bright and sunny influences over it, and from
beneath the frozen surface the lovelier green of kind
and generous natures will appear.

M. De Tocqueville describes the Americans as being
" for the most part strongly influenced by a passion for
gain, and the love of physical comfort, in which chan-
nel men's passions chiefly flow, and sweep away all else
before them. And this spirit," he continues, " is frequently combined with a kind of religious morality,—
an attempt to make the *most of this world, without
losing the next.* There are few great designs,—petty
objects and pleasures of the day engross much of their
attention."

The American women are in general religious and
highly moral; "and women are the guardians of morality. If I were asked to what I would principally
attribute the singular prosperity and increasing power
of the American people, I would reply, to the superiority of the females of that nation. Whilst the European *endeavours to forget his domestic troubles by
agitating society,* the American derives from his home

M

that love of order which he afterwards carries with him into public affairs."—DE TOCQUEVILLE, *Part* 2.

If peace, happiness, and the love of order, reign within a man's own breast, and within his domestic circle, his intercourse with society will be useful and beneficent. But the slave of evil passions endeavours to make others as discontented and turbulent as himself; and that is the hidden source of much political agitation which sets the world in commotion.

> Friend, parent, neighbour, first it will embrace,
> His country next, and next all human race.

When M. De Tocqueville speaks of the domestic troubles and discomfort of Europeans, we may presume he takes his idea of them from his native France, or from other countries with which he is most familiar. The same high character which he has given to the American females, is justly due to their fair sisters in the British isles, whence the American ladies have their origin. HOME is one of the most charming words in their common language; and to many of us it is the best beloved spot the sun shines upon.

"The Americans," says Mr. Dickens, "are by nature frank, brave, cordial, hospitable, and affectionate. Cultivation and refinement seem but to enhance their warmth of heart and ardent enthusiasm; and it is the possession of these latter qualities, in a most remarkable degree, which renders an educated American one of the most endearing and most generous of friends. I never was so won upon as by this class; never yielded up my full confidence and esteem so readily and pleasurably as to them; never can make again, in half a year, so many friends, for whom I seem to entertain the regard of half a life. These qualities are natural, I implicitly believe, to the whole people. That they are, however, sadly sapped and blighted in their growth among the mass, and that there are influences at work which endanger them still more, and give but little present promise of their healthful restoration, is a truth that ought to be told."

One of those evil influences is extreme distrust, especially with regard to public men; a propensity which adds to the mischievous power of a false and scurrilous press, abridges and embitters the career of the best statesmen, throws places of trust and authority into the hands of an inferior class of aspirants, and infects the whole course of affairs with the spirit of change. " Is this well ?" observes the same writer, " or likely to elevate the character of the governors or the governed? The answer is invariably the same : ' There's freedom of opinion here, you know. Every man thinks for himself; and we are not to be easily over-reached. That's how our people come to be suspicious.'......The love of trade is assigned as a reason for that comfortless custom so very prevalent in country towns, of married persons living in hotels, having no fire-side of their own, and seldom meeting from early morning until late at night, but at the hasty public meals. The love of trade is a reason why the literature of America is to remain for ever unprotected: ' for we are a trading people, and don't care for poetry,' though we do, by the way, profess to be very proud of our poets; while healthful amusements, cheerful means of recreation, and wholesome fancies, must fade before the stern utilitarian joys of trade."

Corroding care follows them even on board the steam ships,* where " all the passengers are very dismal, and seem to have tremendous secrets weighing on their minds..........You might suppose the whole male portion of the company to be the melancholy ghosts of

---

* Scandit æratas vitiosa naves cura !

departed book-keepers, who had fallen dead at the desk:
such is their weary air of business and calculation."—
DICKENS's *American Notes.*

But is there not some cause to guard against the
increase of the same spirit in our own country? Is
there not a growing disposition among us to encourage
and prosecute trade at all hazards, without duly considering the consequences to agriculture, to health,
morals, intellectual, and social improvement? Happiness is what all men desire, and as means to that end
many are covetous of gain, and of a greater share of
political power, or, as they imagine, of more liberty.
But here is proof that a man's life and real enjoyment
consist not in the abundance of these things.

It is curious and important to observe the comparative
influence of monarchy and democracy, as regards the
distinctions of rank, the outward signs and emblems of
official dignity, the habits and manners of a people.

The French during the last century were perhaps
the most polished nation in Europe. At the Revolution the manners of the people became fierce and
brutal, and they have ceased to be polite and agreeable,
as they formerly were.

The dogma of universal equality, according to which
the American President is the servant of the sovereign
people, deprives him of all regal shew and pomp. The
judges and barristers usually dispense with the robes
and other badges of their profession and office. The
author of "Men and Manners in America," (Captain
Hamilton,) observed in the supreme court of the state
of New York, that when the jurymen delivered their
verdict, three-fourths of them were eating bread and
cheese, and the foreman announced it with his mouth
full, uttering the disjointed syllables during the inter-
vals of mastication.

In England, our just laws secure to masters and ser--

vants equal rights: the moral code must do the rest. In well regulated households, an old and faithful servant is the friend of the family; he shares in their happiness, and sorrows for their afflictions. He has done his duty honestly and respectfully, and his master and mistress treat him in return with respect and kindness. The children are attached to him, for they remember how he delighted in their youthful sports, and the cheerful smile with which he welcomed them back from school; how their good conduct and their rewards made him glad, how grieved he was for their disgrace and punishment. When old and grey-headed, the faithful English servant has friends and benefactors that will not forsake him; and if the number of such male and female servants is decreasing, it is no sign of our improvement, but the contrary. They are singularly free from cares, losses, and hardships; for both in prosperous and adverse times their wants are supplied; and many an one has had cause to regret leaving a good place and comfortable home, to undertake the maintenance of a family, and encounter the anxieties and risks of trade.

A bad master cannot expect to retain a good and valuable servant; neither can a bad servant hope to enjoy the confidence and esteem of a good master. But kind, considerate, and judicious management on the one hand, and fidelity and diligence on the other, produce that mutual respect and attachment, and that harmony and happiness, which we often see in this kingdom, where the reciprocal duties of heads of families and their households are performed, from the best and highest motives.

The recollection of some who read these pages will supply not a few pleasing instances in which this important and interesting relationship has subsisted for many years on the happiest footing. I confine myself to a single example.

The following is the inscription over a recent grave in a churchyard in Somersetshire.

Sacred to the Memory

OF

ELIZABETH BARKER,

WHO FROM EARLY YOUTH TILL DEATH, SERVED THE MEMBERS

OF ONE FAMILY WITH CONSCIENTIOUS ZEAL

AND DEVOTED ATTACHMENT.

SHE DIED AT WESTON-SUPER-MARE, OCTOBER 1, 1842,

AGED FIFTY-THREE,

IN THE SERVICE OF MRS. ————,

WHO HAS INSCRIBED THIS MEMORIAL OF ESTEEM AND

AFFECTIONATE REGARD.

" Thou hast been faithful over a few things."—MATT. xxv. 23.

Partly from the readiness with which the Americans can find other employment, and partly from republican independence, they generally avoid the situation of domestic servants. Those who do undertake it call themselves " helps." But the help they give is so precarious—they are so ready to fly off, the moment they find it convenient or feel dissatisfied, that were it not for the Irish emigrants and negroes, the wealthier Americans would often be obliged to help themselves.

Men are strangely inconsistent, for the very individual who would disdain to perform the proper duties of a respectable servant, or to take the name of one, will go with his earnings into the southern states, and purchase one or more of his fellow-creatures, whose complexion the sun has blackened, whom he will compel to wait on him and work for him, as a servant of servants, or slave. This is all wrong. The Bible gives us a very different view of the matter. " For whether is greater, he that sitteth at meat, or he that serveth? Is not he that sitteth at meat? But I am among you as he that serveth." Here is Divine dignity and con-

descension! What but the littleness of human pride
leads a man to deem himself degraded by that condition in which Providence has placed him, when He
who has " a name above every name, took upon himself
the form of a servant," and from that voluntary lowli-
ness was highly exalted.

Miss Martineau, who appears to have a strong love of
democracy, states, as the result of her observation in
America, that " where a complete mutual understanding
is arrived at, there is the best chance of the terms of the
contract being faithfully adhered to, and liberally con-
strued on both sides : and I have seen instances of the
parties having lived together in friendship and contentment, for five, seven, eleven, and fourteen years. Others,
again, I have seen, who, without fault of their own,
have changed their servants three times in a fortnight.
Some, too, I have observed, who will certainly never
be comfortably settled, unless they can be taught the
first principles of democracy. ( ! )

" All American ladies should know how to clear-
starch and iron ; how to keep plate and glass ; how to
cook dainties ; and if they understand the making of
bread and soup likewise, so much the better. The
gentlemen usually charge themselves with the business
of marketing, which is very fair. A lady, highly
accomplished and very literary, told me that she had
lately been left entirely without help, in a country
village where there was little hope of being speedily
able to procure any. She and her daughter made the
bread, for six weeks, and entirely kept the house, which
might vie with any nobleman's for true luxury, perfect
sufficiency, and neatness.

" A country lady travelled thirty miles, to a town
where she thought she might intercept some Irish,
coming down from Canada into the States, and supply
herself with domestics from among them. She engaged

to send them thirty miles to confession, twice a year, if they would live with her.

" Another country lady told me that her family suffered from want of water, because the man objected to bring it. The maids fetched it; and even the children in their little cans. The man was sturdy on the point, and she could not dismiss him for such a reason, he was such a valuable servant; though he could not drive, from having only one eye, and always got drunk when his work was done.

" The mother of a young bride of my acquaintance flattered herself that she had graced her daughter's new house, during the wedding journey, with two exemplary domestics. The day previous to the bride's return, before the women had seen either master or mistress, they gave notice that they were going away directly, in consequence of the receipt of some family news, which had changed their plans. They were prevailed upon to stay for a week, when they persisted in going, though no successors had been obtained, and their young mistress was to receive her company the next day. What made the matter desperate was, that the bride knew nothing of housekeeping. She made them cook as much provision, to be eaten cold, as would possibly keep; and when they had closed the door behind them, sat down and cried for a whole hour. How she got out of her troubles, I forget; but she was in excellent spirits when she told me the story.

" A young man from Vermont was hired by a family who were in extreme want of a footman. He was a most friendly personage, as willing as he was free and easy; but he knew nothing of life out of a small farm-house. An evening or two after his arrival, there was a large party at the house. His mistress strove to impress upon him, that all he had to do at tea-time was to follow, with sugar and cream, the waiter who carried the tea; to see that every one had tea and sugar, and to hold his tongue. He did his part with an earnest face, stepping industriously from guest to guest. When he had made the circuit and reached the door, a doubt struck him whether a group in the farthest part of the room had had the benefit of his attentions. He raised himself on his toes with, ' I'll ask;' and shouted over the heads of the company, ' I say, how are ye off for sweetenin' in that ere corner?' "—Miss Martineau's *Society in America.*

In America, democratic pride has rejected the names of master or servant, although they are both found in the Bible, and their mutual duties are fully enjoined there. The servants gratify their feelings by calling themselves " helps," and their masters " bosses."

Mr. Fearon says, " A friend of mine the other day met with a rebuff at his hotel, which taught him the necessity of altering, not his ideas indeed, but his words. Addressing the female help, he said, ' Be kind enough to tell your mistress that I should be glad to see her.' ' My mistress, Sir! I tell you I have no mistress, nor master either. I will not tell her, Sir, I guess. If you want Mrs. M. you may go to her yourself, I guess. In this country there is no mistresses nor masters. I guess I am a woman citizen.' "

It is rather strange to compare the independent tone of style and sentiment of this woman citizen, this chamber help at an hotel, with that of the President of the United States, Gen. Harrison, who, in his inaugural address, as quoted in the preceding lecture, " described himself as the accountable agent, not the principal—the servant, not the master." So the President is the servant, not the boss of the sovereign people,—not even their help.

And on these principles, every citizen, provided he be not a negro, may attend the President's levee, may shake his hand, and drink his punch, as if he were as good and great a man as he. The author of " Men and Manners in America," (Captain Hamilton) thus describes the levee of the President, General Jackson, at Washington.

" There were present at this levee men begrimed with all the filth accumulated in their day's—perhaps their week's labour. There were sooty artificers evidently fresh from the forge or the workshop; and one individual I remember,—either a miller or a baker,— who, wherever he passed, left marks of contact on the garments of the company. The most prominent group however in the assemblage, was a party of Irish labourers, employed on some neighbouring canal, who had evidently been apt scholars in the doctrine of liberty and equality, and were determined, on the present occasion, to assert the privileges of 'the great unwashed.' I remarked these men pushing aside the more respectable portion of the company with a certain jocular audacity which put one in mind of the humours of Donnybrook.

" A party composed of the materials I have described could possess but few attractions. The heat of the apartment was very great, and the odours (certainly not Sabæan) which occasionally affected the nostrils were more pungent than agreeable. .........

" During the time I was engaged at the levee, my servant remained in the hall through which lay the entrance to the apartments occupied by the company, and on the day following he gave me a few details of a scene somewhat extraordinary, but sufficiently characteristic to merit record. It appeared that the refreshments intended for the company, consisting of punch and lemonade, were brought by the servants with the intention of reaching the interior saloon. No sooner, however, were these ministers of Bacchus descried to

be approaching by a portion of the company, than a
rush was made from within, the whole contents of the
trays were seized *in transitu*, by a sort of *coup de main*;
and the bearers (having thus rapidly achieved the distribution of their refreshments) had nothing for it but
to return for a fresh supply. This was brought and
quite as compendiously despatched, and at length it
became apparent that without resorting to some extraordinary measures, it would be impossible to accomplish
the intended voyage, and the more respectable part of
the company would be suffered to depart with dry
palates, in utter ignorance of the extent of the hos-
pitality to which they were indebted.

"The butler, however, was an Irishman; and in
order to baffle further attempts at intercepting the
supplies, had recourse to an expedient marked by all
the ingenuity of his countrymen. He procured an
escort, armed them with sticks; and on his next
advance these men kept flourishing their shillelahs
around the trays with such alarming vehemence, that
the predatory horde, who anticipated a repetition of
their plunder, were scared from their prey, and amid
a scene of execrations and laughter, the refreshments,
thus guarded, accomplished their journey to the saloon
in safety!"

This having happened, it would seem that there is
nothing to prevent it from happening again. Still it
would be unfair to suppose that all the President's
levees are of this character. Mr. Dickens gives a much
more favourable description of one of President Tyler's
levees which he attended.

"The great drawing-room, which I have already
mentioned, and the other chambers on the ground-
floor were crowded to excess. The company was not,
in our sense of the term, select, for it comprehended
persons of very many grades and classes; nor was

there any great display of costly attire; indeed some of the costumes may have been, for aught I know, grotesque enough. But the decorum and propriety of behaviour which prevailed were unbroken by any rude or disagreeable incident; and every man, even among the miscellaneous crowd in the hall who were admitted without any orders or tickets, to look on, appeared to feel that he was a part of the institution, and was responsible for its preserving a becoming character, and appearing to the best advantage."

And of President Jackson's levee, above referred to, Capt. Hamilton says, " During my stay at Washington, I never heard it mentioned without an expression of indignant feeling on the part of the ladies at the circumstances I have narrated. Yet the evil, whatever be its extent, is in truth the necessary result of a form of government essentially democratic."

The American ladies were perfectly right in their judgment, and we may congratulate ourselves that the London sweeps and bakers, and the labourers on railways, are not permitted to rush into the levees and drawing-rooms at St. James's, covered with soot, meal, and mud; and that the Queen is guarded from intrusion to which no good subject, whatever be his station, would wish to expose her Majesty. Such familiarity may produce contempt, and contempt for persons in authority is the first step to disobedience and rebellion. To ascribe undue importance to forms and ceremonies is weak and childish; to dispense with them altogether is unwise. In manners, there is the greatest possible difference between a graceful, and a *rude* simplicity.

That decent dignity with which our judges proceed to the assize to administer justice is seemly and becoming the occasion. If we were to see people laughing at a funeral, we should be disgusted with their misbehaviour; and where juries deliver a solemn verdict affecting property, liberty, or life, while they are almost unanimously chewing bread and cheese, not only is there a breach of good manners, but there is danger that persons in authority and that justice herself will be less reverenced.

True politeness is not confined to any station. It may be seen in the peasant and the artizan, and it may be wanting in the hollow-hearted courtier, or the coxcomb who affects the manners of the great; but it is always inconsistent with coarse and presumptuous familiarity. In the happiest families, parents know how to love their children with the warmest affection; but without losing respect and authority. And the most intimate friendship cannot subsist without a regard to the same rules.

> The man that hails you Tom or Jack,
> And proves, by thumps upon your back,
>   How he esteems your merit,
> Is *such* a friend,—that one had need
> Be very much *his* friend indeed,
>   To pardon or to bear it.

Good manners, in short, are the ornament and defence of good morals. Without them, virtue herself would be less lovely and secure. Infinite wisdom has condescended even in this to be our Teacher. The precept, Fear God, is combined with the commands, Honour all men,—Honour the King. We are not only enjoined to be pitiful, but also to be courteous.

The American boys are republicans from early childhood, and experiments have actually been made to ascertain how far a strictly republican government would be admissible in schools.* The school were

---

* "Such a method was adopted at an institution for boys, denominated the Gardiner Lyceum, in the state of Maine. Such institutions have succeeded for a time, when the prin-

allowed to elect, by universal suffrage, eight or ten
boys, who were invested with the legislative power, and
held their deliberations once a week, for the management of scholastic affairs. The master and his assist-
ants had only a *veto* or negative on their proceedings.
They could pardon, but not punish. In this young
republic, it soon appeared that the legislative power had
a very strong tendency to absorb the executive;—that
the *master*, like the American President,—was *not* the
master; and that the people and their representatives
in the legislature, prevented him from wielding the
schoolmaster's rod of empire with such vigour, as was
necessary to produce a salutary and lasting impression.
Whatever might have been the proficiency of the
scholars in democratical science,—and in those accom-
plishments that are best learned during holidays and
half holidays,—somehow they did not make equal progress in grammatical, arithmetical, geographical, and
mathematical learning. And so it was found expedient
to change the form of government, into one more nearly
resembling that which has been most approved, since
the days of Solomon.*

From our rapid survey of the political institutions of
two great nations, descended from the same ancestry,
but placed in different hemispheres, it is evident that
both enjoy a large measure of freedom and felicity, the

cipal has possessed a sufficient share of *generalship* to enable
him really to manage the institution *himself*, while the power
has been left *nominally* in the hands of the boys. Should
this not be the case, as Mr. Abbott judiciously remarks, and
should the institution actually be surrendered into the hands
of the boys, things must be on a very unstable footing. And
accordingly even in republican America, wherever such a
plan has been adopted, it has in every instance been abandoned, and a more aristocratic system established in its
room."—CASWALL'S *America*, 1839.

         * Prov. xxii. and xxiii.

one under a limited monarchy, the other as a republic. They have some advantages in common, and some that are peculiar to each.

Hence we may learn to distrust those cold and severe dogmatists, who undertake to calculate and adjust human liberty and happiness according to one fixed scale for every meridian of the globe, regardless of local and national peculiarities, customs, manners, genius, sentiment, the graces and the proprieties of life. They reason as if they would not hesitate to uproot and level the old societies, in order to carry out their sweeping theory of democracy all over the world.*

But in England we enjoy, as the Americans also do, the right of administering our own local affairs; the power of going where we please, and doing what is lawful, untroubled by spies and arbitrary interference. Under those admirable laws and judicial institutions of England which the Americans have wisely adopted, our persons and property, our liberty and lives are safe. The rights of conscience are respected, and all sects are tolerated, except atheists and blasphemers,— the enemies of all law and all religion. Here then is rational practical freedom, in those things that chiefly concern our welfare, and come home to our business and bosoms.

In comparing our constitution with that of the great modern republic, it was proved that the British empire could not exist as a democracy; nor retain its own great and signal advantages, grasping at the same time those which the Americans possess under very different circumstances and institutions. Having considered the probable effect of the introduction of the ballot, universal suffrage, annual parliaments, of the abolition of our hereditary peerage and hereditary mo-

See page 62.

narchy, we found that so to intermix our iron with clay would incongruously weaken the whole constitutional fabric, and hasten its fall.

The establishment of the American union of republics, in a vast and unlimited territory in the new world, was coeval with an attempt to erect democracy amid the crash and wreck of an ancient kingdom, in the centre of Europe. France, far unlike England, was greatly misgoverned. But instead of aiming to improve their government wisely, gradually, and lawfully, the French revolutionists set up the wild cry of liberty and equality, and rushed forward in a career, from which the best and most moderate, who had hoped for rational freedom without the destruction of existing establishments, would have shrunk back with horror, could they have foreseen the disorder and havoc that ensued.

The first leaders of the movement were hurried on impetuously to participate in crimes which they could not prevent. They were soon pushed aside or trampled down, to make way for atheists, murderers, regicides, who, when society had been stirred to its darkest depths, came up to rule by the torch, the dagger, and the guillotine. They worshipped the image of departed liberty. The wicked were unchained : fair France became a place of prisons and massacres, a field of blood, a land of discord, obscenity, and profaneness. Infuriated anarchists, in the pride of their perverted reason, like men possessed with devils, stalked fiercely among fragments of desolation and the tombs of the slain, and no man could bind them. The civilized world stood aghast at the tremendous spectacle. Without that agitation of spirit which overwhelmed the first spectators, we, at the distance of more than half a century, can view, in every part and in its full dimensions, that awful scene. Yet there are some for whom it has been transacted and recorded in vain; for still they would

not hesitate, with unteachable folly, to plunge headlong through the same errors and calamities to a similar
catastrophe.

Under the best government, full and constant employment cannot always be obtained, for a numerous
manufacturing and agricultural population, with uninterrupted peace and plenty. But turbulence aggravates
those evils, by rendering property insecure, and interfering with the regular employment of capital and labour.
Any system that should raise to power men of inferior
principle and capacity, instead of removing those ills
which a good government in tranquil times may alle-
viate, would multiply our disorders and distresses ten-
fold.

Liberty has been the darling theme of poets and
orators; and doubtless the love of it is ennobling, when
founded on a patriotic attachment to wise, good, and
venerable institutions that have stood the test of experience; and when it consists in a righteous indignation against flagrant injustice, oppression, and slavery.
When Buonaparte had brought many nations under
his yoke, and was preparing his armaments against
this island, we believed and we felt that our homes and
altars were well worth defending; domestic troubles
were forgotten; strife was hushed; one pervading sentiment animated every breast; and one strong desire
nerved every arm to drive back the tyrant's legions
from the British strand.

> By oppression's woes and pains,
> By our sons in servile chains,
> We will drain our dearest veins,
> But they shall be free.

Then a great nation's mighty heart throbbed with that
generous emotion,—the love of liberty,—dearer than
life, which impelled all her true sons to prolong the

death-struggle rather than survive her ruin.    But
was it the same liberty which they idolatrously worshipped in the Champs de Mars and throughout France,
when her infatuated people swore to adhere for ever to
the constitution planned by their national convention,
—a constitution which lasted one short year ?    Was it
the liberty in whose name so many crimes have been
committed ?    No more so, than vile hypocrisy is true
religion.    The liberty of mob orators and anarchists is
impatience of controul and lust of power.    It is the
self-same passion that we should mightily resist in a
military tyrant,—the robber and spoiler of nations.
The political incendiary must gloss over his ambitious
projects with the fair names of freedom, and of zeal for
the people's good ; for he is not able to persuade with
vollies of musketry and the deep-mouthed cannon.
But "the tongue is a little member and boasteth great
things.    Behold how great a matter a little fire kindleth.
And the tongue is a fire, a world of iniquity,—and
setteth on fire the course of nature."    With that he
kindles the pride, the discontent, the contentious spirit,
smouldering in many a breast.    He seduces to his
standard his country's fretful and rebellious sons.    He
beguiles them with false motives and delusive hopes;
he chafes them into fury.    They burn, they glow, but
not with the pure flame of heaven-descended liberty:

> For whence,
> But from the author of all ill, could spring
> So deep a malice. . . . . . . . . . . .
> For neither do the spirits damn'd
> Lose all their virtue ; lest bad men should boast
> Their specious deeds on earth, which glory excites
> Or close ambition, varnish'd o'er with zeal.

Those restless longings after absolute freedom, what
are they, but the cravings of the unsatisfied soul that
has missed its road to happiness ?    Perfect liberty is

never to be enjoyed but in union with perfect virtue, unattainable here, though striven after by the wise and good, and seen radiant with surpassing glory, in the bright vista of immortality.

But those that with steadfast feet pursue, although imperfectly, the liberty they hope for, clamour not for equal rights, nor goad the heady multitude to treason's brink, nor urge them headlong down the steep, to ruin. None but the Divine government is perfect. When that which we supplicate, "Thy kingdom come, thy will be done on earth, as it is in heaven," *shall* come, then only will exist entire obedience to a perfect law, which is true happiness and true liberty. The systems of all human lawgivers, necessarily imperfect in theory, must be still more so in practice. The government of nations is therefore at best an endeavour to overcome evil with good. Happy are the people whose political constitution is on the whole well adapted to their circumstances, character, customs, and real welfare. Still happier are they, who possessing such advantages, have the wisdom to value and the power to preserve them from violent changes and convulsions, which must ever occasion incalculable suffering, and endanger, if not destroy, true freedom. The first British colonists in North America well defined it to be " the liberty of doing, without fear, all that is *just and good;*" and Montesquieu says that "political liberty does not consist in an unrestrained freedom. In governments, that is, in societies directed by laws, liberty can consist only in the power of doing what we ought to will, and in not being constrained to do what we ought not to will." Very different is the democratic idea of liberty, namely, that the people ought to have the power of doing what they please. That indeed would be freedom in a society of angels. But political reformers have too commonly erred, in dealing with men as if they had an

angelic nature, overlooking the characteristic of our
fallen race; the fatal tendency, especially in masses
and bodies of men, to be misled by ignorance, error,
prejudice, and passion. The wise, just, amiable, kind,
and beneficent, are naturally in a minority. Unrestrained freedom would not be liberty, but licentiousness.
It would be worse than despotism—a multitudinous
tyranny, foul and fiend-like.

But we must turn now to a far different theme. A
people that aim to carry freedom to its utmost limits,
nevertheless keep two millions four hundred and ninety
thousand of their fellow creatures, in the midst of their
territory, in slavery. If in America all white men are
assumed to be equal, the coloured race are placed below the common level of humanity. With nature's
indelible brand upon them, they are generally despised
as outcasts and shunned as lepers. England, however,
must take shame to herself, for having introduced this
vicious anomaly into her North American colonies.

The slave trade is unlawful in the United States, although some of the citizens, it is supposed, carry it on
clandestinely. But domestic slavery and the sale of
slaves are allowed and practised. The most favourable
view we can take of its continuance is, that while it is
openly condemned by many of the inhabitants of the
northern states, and secretly disapproved by many
more, the southern states are inured to the evil, and all
are deterred from attempting to get rid of such a blot
on their institutions and their national character, by the
extent of the sacrifice which they apprehend its abolition would involve. The states that hold slaves, and
those that do not, are equal in number; and consequently, one half of the senators represent slave holding
states of the union; and those states take good care to
elect no one favourable to the abolition of slavery, to
any public office.

As already mentioned, the states are entitled by the constitution to send members to the house of representatives, in proportion to the number of their inhabitants. The slaves being more than one sixth part of the whole population, on their account one sixth of that legislative assembly is returned. But whom do those members represent ? whose cause do they plead in Congress ? The interests—the cause of the negroes ? Far otherwise. The negroes are counted as so many men in determining the number of members to be returned to Congress; but they are only reckoned as so much property, when the question is, who are to be their representatives ? In the free institutions of America, the slaves are represented by the owners, who keep them in bondage; and he must be an honest and fearless representative of any state, who dares to plead for their emancipation.

Freedom of speech and debate is a cherished constitutional privilege of the British parliament, declared by statute, (1 Wm. and Mary, st. 2, c. 2.) and essential to liberty. But in the American house of representatives, even the important privilege of freedom of debate is limited, as regards slavery, by the will of the majority, influencing the members of the legislature.

The Washington correspondent of the Boston Atlas newspaper stated in April, 1842, that Mr. Giddings, a representative of Ohio, had the courage and honesty to propose a series of resolutions condemnatory of slavery, and declaring that the territorial law of the slave holding states could not apply to slaves on the high seas,—and that consequently, the slaves on board the Creole, who had gained their liberty and taken the vessel into a British port, in resuming their natural rights of freedom, violated no law of the United States, and were liable to no punishment. Whereupon Mr. Botts, of Virginia, had a resolution proposed, censuring Mr.

Giddings for presuming to advocate the cause of the slaves, and then moved the previous question, in order to prevent Mr. Giddings from being heard. The speaker decided that Mr. Giddings, being accused, had a right to be heard in his defence. But the house of representatives reversed this decision, and adopted the resolution of censure, without giving Mr. Giddings an opportunity of saying one word in his defence. The American writer remarks: " The moment a man from the free states says any thing which touches the subject of slavery, he must be censured by the house. A more direct attempt to destroy freedom of debate was never made in a deliberative assembly. New England herself contributed to this act of despotism, by the votes of the locos of New Hampshire and Maine! O shame, where is thy blush!" There are doubtless many individuals in the northern states, and some few in the south, who are sincerely desirous that slavery should be abolished; but the laws, prejudices, and customs of the country are generally in favour of the negro's degradation.

In Washington, any justice of peace may imprison a negro, and advertise him in the newspapers, that he may be claimed by his owner. Should he be a black who has bought his freedom, might he not assert a free man's rights, and obtain redress in a court of justice? On the contrary, this friendless man may be sold to pay the cost of his own unjust imprisonment. The same is the law in Alabama. It is the common testimony of travellers in America, that in all public places and conveyances, negroes are set apart by themselves; nay, it is even so in the places of worship, as if the soul of a man took its hue from his complexion. Mr. Buckingham says that in a house of refuge for juvenile offenders which he visited, the coloured delinquents were placed in a separate part of the room; no doubt from a tender regard to the exquisite moral feelings and refinement of the white young vagabonds.

The Author of Men and Manners in America mentions that the son of a general of Hayti, a mulatto, of gentlemanly education and manners, accustomed to be treated in his country as became his rank, visited New York, was refused admittance at all the hotels, could only find shelter in a miserable lodging kept by a negro woman, had his money returned by the box keeper at the theatre, who ordered him to go to the upper gallery; and finding that he was every where shunned and rudely treated, he left the United States as soon as possible, in disgust.

It were easy to multiply examples of the cruelty and injustice caused by slavery, and of which we heard enough before it was abolished in our own colonies. Mr. Dickens has made a collection from American newspapers, of advertisements for runaway slaves, giving a painfully graphic view of their maltreatment by masters who abuse their power. Both men and women are described by the iron clogs and collars they wore—by their marks of lashing and burning with a hot iron— by scars and gunshot wounds and mutilation. These business-like announcements for the purpose of recapturing the slaves, tell their tale of misery, in characters engraven on their very bodies, by the hand of the oppressor.

"There are slave auctions," says an author already quoted, "almost every day in the New Orleans Exchange.........One of the first human beings whom I happened to see thus sold, was a poor woman apparently dying of a consumption. She was emaciated, her voice was husky and feeble, and her proper place was evidently the hospital. It was with difficulty she was raised on the table. ' Now, gentlemen, here is Mary,'

said the auctioneer, ' a clever house servant and an
excellent cook. Bid me something for this valuable
lot. She has only one fault, gentlemen, that is,
shamming sick. She pretends to be ill; but there is
nothing more the matter with her, than with me at this
moment. Put her up, gentlemen; shall I say a hundred dollars to begin with ? Well, fifty dollars is bid
for her.' Here the auctioneer stopped, while several
men began feeling the poor woman's ribs, and putting
questions as to her health. ' Are you well ?' asked one
man. ' Oh no, I am very ill.' ' What is the matter
with you ?' ' I have a bad cough and pain in my side.'
' How long have you had it ?' ' Three months and
more.' The auctioneer proceeded :—' Give her a touch
or two of the cow-hide, and I'll warrant she'll do your
work.' She was sold for seventy dollars, amid sundry
jests at the purchaser."

The author most properly remarks, on this disgusting
and disgraceful scene :—" If such scenes are acted in a
Christian country, it is the duty of every traveller to
take care at least, that they shall not be done in a corner, that they shall be proclaimed loudly to the world,
and that those who perpetrate the enormities shall
receive the due meed of indignation and contempt."—
*Men and Manners in America.*

The same writer relates that he travelled in a steam
boat, on the Mississippi, with a slave dealer, whose
gang of slaves were on the deck, the men loaded with
heavy chains, and the women in rags. This slave
dealer's manners were as coarse and brutal as his occupation. " I remember, however, that no one on board
talked *about freedom* so loudly or so long as this slave
dealer. He at length left us, and the sky seemed
brighter, and the earth greener, after his departure."

But slavery exists even at Washington, the seat of
government. " The waiters in the hotels," observes

the same author, " the servants in private families, and
many of the lower classes of artisans are slaves. While
the orators in Congress are rounding periods about
liberty in one part of the city, proclaiming *alto voce*
that all men are equal, and that ' resistance to tyranny
is obedience to God,' the auctioneer is exposing human
flesh to sale in another !"

The demoralizing influence of slavery on the white,
the coloured, and the negro races, is a painful and disgusting subject. There are various details of licentious
depravity given by Miss Martineau, in her chapter on
" Morals of Slavery," which I have no inclination to
repeat.* She states, " Much that is dreadful ensues
from the negro being subject to toil and the lash; but
I am confident that the licentiousness of the masters
is the proximate cause of society in the south and
south-west being in such a state, that nothing else is to
be looked for than its being dissolved into its elements,
if man does not soon cease to be called the property of
man. This dissolution will never take place through
the insurrection of the negroes, but by the natural
operation of vice. It is well known that the most
savage violences that are now heard of in the world,
take place in the southern and western states of
America. Burning alive, cutting the heart out, and
sticking it on the point of a knife, and other such
diabolical deeds, the result of the deepest hatred of

* "Jefferson, continually talking about liberty, brought
his own children to the hammer, and made money of his
debaucheries. Even at his death he did not liberate them.
A daughter of his was sold some years ago by public auction,
at New Orleans, and bought by a society of gentlemen, who
wished to testify, by her liberation, their admiration of the
statesman !"—*Men and Manners in America.*
It may be said, this is dreadful, but surely it is a solitary
example. Miss Martineau, in her " Society in America,"
testifies that such is far from being the case.

which the human heart is capable, are heard of only there." Miss Martineau adds, that there is no dispute as to the existence of such deeds, though their frequency is matter of dispute; but within *thirteen months* of her residence in the United States, she knew of the death of four men by summary burning alive.

In the state of Alabama, the law forbids the teaching of any negro to spell, read, or write, under a penalty of from two hundred and fifty to five hundred dollars; while only two hundred dollars is the penalty for treating a slave with excessive cruelty!

In the New Orleans Picuyane newspaper, of August 12, 1841, the following case was reported.—

"CHAUNCEY B. BLACK.—The charge made on Monday last against this individual, by William H. Avery, was yesterday investigated before Recorder BALDWIN. The accused, it will be recollected, was charged with tampering with the slaves of the complainant, a course of conduct which was calculated to lead to insubordination among them."

Such was the charge, and it was grounded on the fact, that Black, as the agent of a Bible Society, had asked some of Avery's slaves whether they would accept a Bible. That a slave holder should take means for preventing the sacred volume from being distributed among his bondsmen, we can imagine,—bad as such conduct is—but that those who were engaged in such a work should actually make it a principle and rule of their association, to pass by all slaves, as if they had no part or lot in *His* religion who preached liberty to the captive, and the opening of the prison to them that are bound, almost surpasses belief.

" Mr. Maybin, Mr. Lowndes, Mr. Stevens, Mr. Gooderich, the Rev. Mr. Wheaton, and several other *prominent members of the society in question*, were called. From their testimony it appeared, that they

and many other *respectable citizens, of different Protestant denominations,* met in February last, and formed
a society for the distribution of the Bible among the
more destitute members of this community. They
raised a fund of about a thousand dollars, and sent an
order to New York for a lot of Bibles equal in value to
that amount, directing that some of them be printed in
English, some in French, some in Spanish, and some in
the German language. They received them in June,
and appointed agents from among their members to
have them placed in proper hands; *but it never for a
moment entered into the minds of the society to present
a single Bible to a slave.*

"Mr. Lowndes impressed it strongly on the minds
of the court, that before any Bibles were distributed to
the parties whose names might be taken by the accused,
the list was to be first submitted to him, *and as it was
opposed to his own feeling, and contrary to the intention of the society, he would certainly furnish no slaves
with a Bible!*

"The strongest and most satisfactory proof was given,
that the accused bore an excellent character, and that,
in speaking to the slaves at all, he acted from a mis-
conception of Mr. Lowndes' instructions, and an ignorance of his duty as a *sub-agent of the Bible Society.*

"After the testimony was heard, the counsel for the
accused, Mr. Micon, said, he trusted the Recorder,
having heard the evidence, would see the propriety of
at once discharging his client, and would not send him
*before the criminal court.* He then argued that the
fact of asking a slave, ' Can you read or write ? will
you take a Bible ?' of which his client was unwittingly
guilty, does not come within the purview of the statute,
which makes it punishable to do any act which would
lead to insubordination among the slaves.

"The Recorder addressed the prisoner, and told him

that he highly approved the laudable work, distributing the Bible, in which he was engaged; but while executing the duty, he must be cautious that he does not infringe on other rights which *are as dear to this community as religion itself.* Believing that in speaking to the slaves he was actuated by no evil intention, he would discharge him, bidding him God speed in his religious career, and cautioning him against bringing himself in *contact with our institutions.*"

No narrative that I ever read of auctions, or bonds, or stripes, or imprisonment, so deeply impressed me with the conviction that slavery is an utterly accursed thing, as this trial, considering the nature of the charge, the evidence of the exculpatory witnesses, the defence of the accused by his counsel, and the opinion of the judge. What contamination, produced by a vicious principle! How unlike the Divine Author of our religion, to turn away from the poor bondsman, to keep back the charter of salvation, from those for whom the Saviour purchased spiritual freedom.

> He is the freeman, whom the truth makes free,
> And all are slaves beside.
>        The oppressor holds
> His body bound, but knows not what a range
> His spirit takes, unconscious of a chain.

But the judge who exhorts these Americans to persevere in their laudable endeavours to promote the religious improvement of white men, conspires with them to keep the African enslaved both in body and soul. What institutions must those be which need such protection? The occasion would justify the severest, the most indignant invective. But rather let us forbear, and pity the master as well as his slave.

Our American brethren have still a canker in their institutions, which strikes upwards and downwards its virulence. It is more blessed to give than to receive. It is more accursed to oppress than to be oppressed.

To us it is a cause for lively gratitude, that we are thus tempted to do unjustly no longer, since throughout the British dominions slavery is no more; that we enjoy freedom of opinion and the rights of conscience without respect of persons; that our just laws, which punish none but criminals, guard alike, from the fraud and violence of the wicked, the property, the persons, the liberty, of masters and servants, of the rich and the poor.

The savage Indians seem to have been the appointed tenants of the North American wilderness, till the arrival of a more highly favoured race, who were to change both the material and the moral aspect of that great continent. Multitudes of their wandering tribes have perished by a mysterious doom; and in the course of two centuries, a mighty nation, sprung from British ancestors, have peopled those immense solitudes, and are still rapidly changing the desert into fruitfulness by the onward resistless march of civilization. Can Englishmen consider their past history, their present condition, and their future destiny, without the deepest interest?

That our forefathers used the American colonists wrongfully, that they have heretofore requited those wrongs with a brother's resentment, more bitter than that of a stranger, was a melancholy proof of our common frailty. But a brighter and happier day has arisen now; and when we look above and beyond the jealousies of rival nations, to the grand and allwise designs of the almighty Ruler,—when we see that *kindred* race multiplying as the stars of heaven and the dust of the earth, overspreading the new world with our lineage, our laws, and our religion, we cherish the hope that strife and enmity shall expire on the altars of peace—

that Ephraim shall not envy Judah, and Judah shall not vex Ephraim—that in ages to come, the descendants of the Indian warrior, the enslaved African, and the freeborn Briton, shall mingle together united and free, because God hath made them so, and the once silent wilderness be vocal with His praise.

END OF LECTURES.

# ADDITIONAL NOTES.

THE effect of the President's suspensive veto is more fully and correctly stated at page 91, than in giving the outline of the American constitution at page 34, where there is a slight inaccuracy which escaped observation until the first sheets had been printed.

Many of the working classes attended these lectures, and the author has had some pleasing proofs of their intelligent interest in the inquiry, by which he is encouraged to hope that should this volume find its way into some factories and workshops, it may be the means of promoting among our industrious and skilful artizans such sentiments as are expressed in the following extract of a letter from one of their number:—

"Honoured Sir,—I was taught, in my childhood, to love my country, its sovereign, its religion, and its laws, I always loved it, I loved it when I entered the Assembly Room on last Monday evening. But, Sir, when I left that room, that love was greatly enhanced; and had not prudence forbid it, I should have let loose the strength of my voice, and the audience must have heard from me,

England, with all thy faults, I love thee still.

And Sir, may the blessings of the God of our nation still rest on her; and may that Divine hand, which has so mercifully saved her amidst wars and difficulties past, still preserve her from internal commotion, and from foreign foes. Sir, I feel more than ever determined to disseminate a spirit of patriotism wherever and whenever opportunity may be afforded me of so doing.

"Most honoured Sir, I most humbly hope you will pardon my thus presuming; it arises from the *warmth of my heart,* and throw myself on your clemency touching all imperfections, being but an humble mechanic.

"Begging to subscribe myself, &c."

J. Chilcott. Printer. Wine Street, Bristol.

www.ingramcontent.com/pod-product-compliance
Lightning Source LLC
Chambersburg PA
CBHW031159270326
41931CB00006B/336